DEUTERONOMY

The Book of Love

Other Books by Jiří Moskala

Edited Books

Christ, Salvation, and the Eschaton: Essays in Honor of Hans K. LaRondelle
(Daniel Heinz, Jiří Moskala, and Peter M. van Bemmelen, editors)

The Cosmic Battle for Planet Earth: Essays in Honor of Norman R. Gulley
(Ronald A. G. du Preez and Jiří Moskala, editors)

Creation, Life, and Hope: Essays in Honor of Jacques B. Doukhan

God's Character and the Last Generation
(Jiří Moskala and John C. Peckham, editors)

Meeting With God on the Mountains: Essays in Honor of Richard M. Davidson

Authored Books

Ezra and Nehemiah

The Laws of Clean and Unclean Animals of Leviticus 11

The Book of Daniel and the Maccabean Thesis (Czech)

The Gospel According to Moses (Czech)

Gospel for Today (Czech)

In the Kingdom of the Messiah (Czech)

DEUTERONOMY

The Book of Love

Jiří Moskala

Pacific Press®
Publishing Association
Nampa, Idaho | www.pacificpress.com

Cover design and illustration by Lars Justinen

Library of Congress Cataloging-in-Publication Data

Names: Moskala, Jiří, author.
Title: Deuteronomy, the book of love / Jiří Moskala.
Description: Nampa, Idaho : Pacific Press Publishing Association, [2021] | Includes bibliographical references. | Summary: "Deuteronomy, The Book of Love is a review of the primary themes of the fifth book of the Bible. It shows how Deuteronomy expands on God's previous revelation, providing practical advice on how the Israelites are to live in the new territory He is giving them. It also reminds them to revere God and maintain a loving and obedient relationship with him"— Provided by publisher.
Identifiers: LCCN 2021003873 (print) | LCCN 2021003874 (ebook) |
ISBN 9780816367504 (paperback) | ISBN 9780816367511 (ebook)
Subjects: LCSH: Bible. Deuteronomy—Criticism, interpretation, etc. | God—Worship and love—Biblical teaching. | God—Love—Biblical teaching.
Classification: LCC BS1275.52 .M67 2021 (print) | LCC BS1275.52 (ebook) | DDC 222/.1506—dc23
LC record available at https://lccn.loc.gov/2021003873
LC ebook record available at https://lccn.loc.gov/2021003874

June 2021

Contents

Introduction

Setting the Stage

The book of Deuteronomy is the book of love. This may be a surprising statement, but I am convinced it is true. Consider the following facts: Moses, in his address to Israel, notes that "the LORD loves you" (Deuteronomy 7:8). God's love and how we should love Him are expressed more emphatically in the book of Deuteronomy than anywhere else in the Pentateuch—or even the entire Hebrew Bible. It is in Deuteronomy that Revelation, for the first time, uses the noun *love* to express the Lord's love for humans. The Hebrew noun translated as "love"—*'ahabah*—is used forty times in the Old Testament, but only five times does it describe God's love (Deuteronomy 7:8; Isaiah 63:9; Jeremiah 31:3; Hosea 11:4; Zephaniah 3:17). The Hebrew verb translated as "love"—*'ahab*—is employed twenty-two times in the book of Deuteronomy, and six times it designates God's love toward people (Deuteronomy 4:37; 7:13; 10:15, 18; 23:5; 33:3). Just in this one book, in Moses' preaching to the people, he stresses seven times that God loves humans! So that the people will never forget this, Moses emphasizes that God is for them and never against them. The book of Deuteronomy is really about love. In addition to these seven occurrences, God's covenant of love is mentioned twice by Moses (Deuteronomy 7:9, 12), even though he uses the term *khesed* ("steadfast love"), which is a synonymous Hebrew word for "love."

On the other hand, Moses strongly exhorts believers to love God because this is the only proper response to the God of love. We love God because He first loved us (1 John 4:19). Ten times Moses exhorts Israel to love God (Deuteronomy 6:5; 10:12; 11:1, 13, 22; 13:3; 19:9; 30:6, 16, 20) and underlines that God blesses those who love Him (Deuteronomy 5:10; 7:9).

Students of the Bible usually think that Deuteronomy is all about the law—a "second law," or a "repetition of the law," as the term *Deuteronomy* indicates. Unfortunately, this inserted title is deeply misleading because the book is not primarily about commands and laws. Rather, it is about God's positive attitude toward His people and their response of love toward Him. It is this love that was on the heart of Moses as he expressed his farewell to God's people—a people called and chosen by the Lord to be His followers and a light to the world.

Please acquaint yourself with the structure of the book of Deuteronomy (see the appendix) in order to comprehend the overall message and themes of the book. This knowledge will guide you in understanding and interpreting each section in its context and will help you to see the flow of thoughts and the big picture of God's revelation of love.

The importance of the book of Deuteronomy

The book of Deuteronomy belongs with the most significant literature in the Hebrew Scriptures because it systematically shapes and articulates the faith of God's people in a living God. It is a literary masterpiece, a jewel, and the Magna Carta of Israel's teaching. It is a well-organized document that establishes the Lord's identity and explains how believers should live; it methodically teaches[1] how to properly respond to God's calling. Deuteronomy is a manual of faith and is the religious constitution for God's people, climaxing the Pentateuch and crowning the Torah with a comprehensive meaning of the divine law. These themes are foundational to Judaism and Christianity.

The significance of the book can be supported further by the following facts:

1. Jesus quoted passages from the book of Deuteronomy to defeat Satan's temptations (Matthew 4:1–11). Christ knew this document well, and it was His tool for securing victory over Satan.
2. Deuteronomy is the only book in the Hebrew canon that contains a command to read (*tikra'*) the book (literally, *'et hatorah hazzo't,* meaning "this law"—or, better, "teaching," "direction," or "instruction"). It legislated that the Levites were to read the book to the whole congregation of Israel at the time of the Feast of Tabernacles (Deuteronomy 31:10, 11). God urged Joshua to meditate on God's law both day and night (Joshua 1:8), and this command is a great encouragement for us to do the same. God's blessing comes upon those who practice this, and those who do so are blessed (Psalm 1:1–3). Nothing in the book can be altered, added to, or subtracted (Deuteronomy 4:2; 12:32; compare Revelation 22:18, 19).
3. The greatest commandment is carved into the book of Deuteronomy: "Love the LORD your God with all your heart and with all your soul and with all your strength" (Deuteronomy 6:5, NIV).
4. The fundamental confession of faith regarding monotheism and the uniqueness of God is expressed in Deuteronomy 6:4: "Hear, O Israel: The LORD our God, the LORD is one" (NIV).
5. Deuteronomy is the first systematic theological book ever written about the Lord's identity and the meaning of true faith in the Living God. It contains the essential foundation for doctrines and ethics and is indispensable for an understanding of the Old Testament message. Its crucial themes focus on love, obedience, fear of God, God's law, remembering and forgetting, land, times, festivals, retribution, the divine name, the Lord as a Warrior, the Ten Commandments, and the Shema. In this book, Moses

emphatically called on Israel to reject other gods and worship only the Lord (Deuteronomy 5:8–10; 6:14; 7:25, 26; 12:2–4).

6. This book was so important that Moses asked that it be placed beside the ark of the covenant (Deuteronomy 31:26).
7. The kings of Israel were required to read this book, write it down, learn its teachings, and have it at their disposal by keeping it with them (Deuteronomy 17:18–20), thus showing their devotion, obedience, and dependence upon the ultimate King. The king was not to "turn from the law to the right or to the left" (verse 20 NIV; see also the same command for all the people in Deuteronomy 5:32) because he was to be a model of devotion and obedience.
8. This book had a profound influence on the children of Israel, the ancient community of faith, because their lives in the Promised Land had to be organized according to the instructions presented in it (Deuteronomy 4:40).
9. The Israelites had to write "all the words of this law" (Deuteronomy 27:3, NIV) upon large stones coated with plaster when they crossed the Jordan River and entered the Promised Land (verses 1–8). This ensured that God's instructions and teachings would be remembered and followed by the succeeding generations.
10. The book contains many promises for abundant living and blessings for those who take its teaching to heart. By following its guidelines, the Israelites would gain a deeper understanding of God's will and wisdom. Their devotion would bring them better health and place them ahead of many nations (Deuteronomy 4:6, 36; 5:33; 6:18; 7:15; 11:8). These sacred instructions would provide a blueprint for living a profitable and successful life and, thus, would give the people precise guidance on how to behave (Deuteronomy 4:1, 40; 5:33; 6:2, 24; 8:1; 11:9; 32:47) in order to enjoy the fullness of life. This is why the people needed to "hear" and "obey" God's instructions, which is a frequent theme

in Deuteronomy (Deuteronomy 4:1; 5:1; 6:4; 9:1; 20:3). God's blessings depend upon a deep relationship with Him and obedience to His law. In the Hebrew language, the verb *shama'* means both to "hear" and "obey" because when one hears, it means that such a person understands the issues of life and does what is right and thus follows divine instructions and God's voice (Deuteronomy 4:30; 6:3; 12:28; 27:10; 30:2, 8). The Lord assured the well-being of the children of Israel when they maintained a trusting and obedient relationship with Him.

The purpose of Deuteronomy

The book of Deuteronomy has a double focus. First, it reflects previously revealed biblical messages, and in the process of interpreting the earlier revelation, it begins a new phase by expanding God's instructions and providing practical advice on how to live in the new territory God is about to give Israel. The book looks forward to this different situation—namely, to life in the Promised Land. It anticipates the distinctive conditions of life when the people settle down and fortified towns are built.

The introduction states why the book was written: "Moses began to expound this law" (Deuteronomy 1:5b, NIV). The key Hebrew word in this verse is *ba'ar*, meaning "expound," "interpret," or "make plain." (The same term is also used in Habakkuk 2:2.)

Second, the book of Deuteronomy has the special purpose of teaching God's people to fear the Lord. Moses speaks to the whole nation in order to explain how to revere God and maintain a loving and obedient relationship with Him. This intention is twice underlined in the following key passage: "Gather the people together, men and women and little ones, and the stranger who is within your gates, that they may hear and that they may learn to fear the LORD your God and carefully observe all the words of this law, and that their children, who have not known it, may hear and learn to fear the LORD your God as long as you live in the land which you cross the Jordan to possess" (Deuteronomy 31:12, 13, NKJV). Moses, in his passionate farewell to the children of Israel, states: "Watch out! Be very careful never to forget what you have seen God doing for you. May his miracles have a deep and permanent effect upon your lives! Tell your children and your grandchildren about the glorious miracles he did" (Deuteronomy 4:9, TLB). God does not need to prove Himself to be a gracious, compassionate, and loving Lord because He demonstrates it again and again in the people's daily lives when He brings Israel out of Egypt. His sustaining presence among His people is a breathtaking reality. But they need to see this with fresh eyes because it is so easy to get used to it. They are not to forget His goodness and must always remember how kind He has been to them. The spirit, beauty, and principles of God's law are clearly expressed in Deuteronomy.

Deuteronomy's historical background

The book of Deuteronomy intentionally begins with an affirmative statement: "These are the words that Moses spoke" (Deuteronomy 1:1). The testimony of the book of Deuteronomy points to Moses as its author and identifies its main speaker and writer more than any other book in the Hebrew Scriptures (the name of Moses is used thirty-eight times in the book). Moses is presented in his speaking as well as writing capacity. His writing ministry is well expressed and is underlined in the book (Deuteronomy 28:58; 29:20, 21, 27; 30:10; 31:9–13, 19, 22, 24–26). His writing activity is also explicitly mentioned in other places within the Pentateuch (Exodus 17:14; 24:4; 34:27, 28; Numbers 33:2). This does not exclude the work of an editor(s) or narrator(s) who put the material together and carefully added the account about Moses' death (Deuteronomy 34:5–12) and updated the notes (Deuteronomy 2:10–12, 20–23; 3:9, 11, 13b, 14; 4:41–5:1a; 10:6–9; 27:1a, 9a, 11; 29:1, 2a; 31:1, 2a, 7a, 9, 10a, 14–16a, 22–25, 30; 32:44–46a, 48; 33:1, 2a; 34:1, 4a),[2] and probably not the introduction (Deuteronomy 1:1–5).[3] Moses could have written the book himself (Deuteronomy 31:9, 22, 24) or used a scribe for writing his speeches, song, and blessings. In this case, the best potential candidate for this scribal task would have been Joshua, as he was Moses' assistant during his lifetime (Exodus 24:13; Numbers 11:28; Deuteronomy 1:38; Joshua 1:1) and his successor (Numbers 27:18–23; Deuteronomy 31:7, 8, 23; 34:9). Paul Lawrence completes his outstanding study of second and first millennia BC treaties in comparison to the covenant structure reflected in the book of Deuteronomy with the powerful statement that "there is no compelling reason to reject the traditional view, that Moses was the 'author' of the Pentateuch or at least a very substantial part of it, with Deuteronomy 34, the account of Moses' own death, being a clear exception."[4]

Moses is 120 years old (Deuteronomy 31:2) when he preaches his last three sermons to Israel, commissions Joshua to lead Israel to the Promised Land, composes a final song, and utters a blessing for each of Israel's tribes. Of the generation of those who experienced the Exodus from Egypt, only Moses, Joshua, and Caleb remained alive (plus those people who were children at the time of the Exodus [Numbers 14:28–35]). Thus, the book of Deuteronomy identifies the second generation of those who experienced the Exodus from Egypt (around 1450 BC) as the original audience for Moses' speeches and actions.[5] In this chronology, Moses uttered his three speeches forty years after the Exodus, thus in 1410 BC.

These themes provide the setting for your study of the book of Deuteronomy, giving you the wisdom to live your life for God's glory and learn to be a blessing to those around you. May your meditations on the Word of God fill your heart with new dedication and stir your mind to follow Him faithfully and with joy. Remember, God is faithful. He loves you more than you can imagine, and He wants you to spend eternity with Him. The book of Deuteronomy will help you love, revere, and serve God more deeply, bringing you satisfaction, happiness, and peace.

1. The concept of teaching occurs in Deuteronomy 1:5; 4:1, 5, 9, 10, 14; 5:31; 6:1, 7; 8:3; 11:19; 17:11; 20:18; 24:8; 31:19, 22; 33:10 (mainly using the Hebrew words *lamad*, *yada'*, and *yarah*).

2. For these possible editorial additions, see Daniel I. Block, *The Gospel According to Moses: Theological and Ethical Reflections on the Book of Deuteronomy* (Eugene, OR: Cascade Books, 2012), 30, 31. Block argues that "we hear the voice of the narrator in only sixty-four verses" (72). Some editorial notes are unsettled. For Block's view on how the book of Deuteronomy was put together, see Daniel I. Block, "Recovering the Voice of Moses: The Genesis of Deuteronomy," *Journal of the Evangelical Theological Society* 44, no. 3 (September 2001): 385–408.

3. It is striking that the preamble of the peace treaty between the Egyptian king Ramses II and the Hittite king Hattusili III (1259 BC) has basically the same structure as Deuteronomy 1:1. See Paul Lawrence, *The Books of Moses Revisited* (Eugene, OR: Wipf & Stock, 2011), 67, 68. Also, it is important to note that the Code of Hammurabi (1792–1750 BC) and the Code of Lipit-Ishtar (ca. 1930 BC) have historical prologues that, as is the case with Deuteronomy, play a crucial role in the whole document.

The use of the third person in a narrative does not preclude the writer from being the author and originator of the text. For examples of this feature, see Xenophon's *Anabasis* and Julius Caesar's *The Gallic Wars*.

4. Lawrence, *Books of Moses Revisited*, 123. Lawrence also strongly declares, "If our conclusions are true it is time to leave behind the constraints that the JEDP [Jahwist-Elohist-Deuteromist-Priestly author] Hypothesis places on our understanding of the pentateuchal text. The evidence that we have considered clearly points to the Late Second Millennium BC as the period when the first five books of the Bible were written. So I contend that it is also time to reinstate Moses as the 'author' " (128).

5. For details regarding the date for the Exodus of Israel from Egypt, see William H. Shea, "Exodus, Date of the," in *The International Standard Bible Encyclopedia*, vol. 2, rev. ed., ed. Geoffrey W. Bromiley et al. (Grand Rapids, MI: Eerdmans, 1982), 230–238.

CHAPTER

One

Preamble to Deuteronomy

History is important, but it is more than knowing facts—it is understanding meaning. History is about recognizing streams of thinking, discerning movements in time, and understanding our roots and heritage. It brings perspective on issues and advises our direction in the future. Sacred history is even more crucial than secular history: through it, we recognize God's interventions, His love, and His leadership. In this way, our trust in Him strengthens, and our faith grows. From the flow of history and the acknowledgment of God's past mighty acts, we receive assurance that He will care for us in the future. Even though we do not know the future, we know Him who holds the future, and we can fully trust Him. This is why Ellen G. White's famous statement is so comforting and educational: "We have nothing to fear for the future, except as we shall forget the way the Lord has led us, and His teaching in our past history."[1]

When we do not learn from the past, both personally and corporately, we are doomed to repeat the same mistakes. Without an understanding of human history, we live only for the moment without any orientation in time and perspective. The Bible underlines that those who lack understanding will perish (Psalm 49:20, NIV). The prophet

Hosea confirms this: "A people without understanding will come to ruin" (Hosea 4:14, NIV)! If the memory of God's people is lost, then with it perishes their sense of time, perspective, meaning in life, and knowledge (see more on this point in chapter 10). As we increase our knowledge of the past, we can discern God's glorious purpose for our lives: "God never leads His children otherwise than they would choose to be led, if they could see the end from the beginning and discern the glory of the purpose which they are fulfilling as co-workers with Him."[2]

Historical introduction ✓

The book of Deuteronomy begins by providing the historical background of the events it chronicles. It is significant that the book of Deuteronomy[3] is not a repetition of God's law, previously mentioned in the Pentateuch, nor is it a second or additional law. Rather, it is an interpretation, expansion, and adaptation of God's instructions to the new situation of His people as they transition from a nomadic life in the wilderness to a more urban and settled lifestyle in the new land the Lord had promised to them (Genesis 12:1–3, 7; 13:14–17; 15:18, 19; Exodus 3:8; 6:8; Deuteronomy 1:7, 8). The law of God was now to be applied in Israel's new location.

The reader is positioned in a specific historical situation and time period in order to better understand the message of the book. Deuteronomy 1:1 plainly states, "These are the words which Moses spoke to all Israel on this side of the Jordan in the wilderness, in the plain opposite Suph" (NKJV). Now forty years after the Exodus and the wilderness wanderings, the Israelites are located on the plains of Moab—on the brink of entering the Promised Land. During the last weeks of his earthly life, Moses delivers important messages to God's people: "In the fortieth year, on the first day of the eleventh month, Moses spoke to the people of Israel according to all that the Lord had given him in commandment to them" (verse 3, ESV). The year is now 1410 BC. Let us place this occasion in a broader historical perspective.

The great controversy ✓

Our Seventh-day Adventist understanding of the biblical message is built on the recognition that there is a fierce battle going on between Christ and Satan, good and evil, and light and darkness. This spiritual warfare began in heaven and is embedded as a dominant factor in our theology.[4] A right understanding of the character of God is crucial in this spiritual battle of the great controversy. The foundation stone and all-encompassing truth of our theological system is that God is love (Deuteronomy 7:8; 1 John 4:16). The crucial battle is about understanding who God is. The question is, Whom will we trust? Will we lovingly embrace what God Himself says, or will we believe the devil's propaganda, fake news, and half-truths?

This spiritual war was started in heaven by Lucifer—the anointed cherub who was the most beautiful, wise, and perfect creature of all of God's created beings (Isaiah 14:12; Ezekiel 28:12–15).[5] After some time (we do not know exactly when), he accused God of not being a loving, fair, and just God but a tyrant who takes away our freedom by His stringent commandments and demands for absolute obedience (Genesis 3:1–10). The anointed cherub who should have protected God's law, secured His government, and guarded the order (in the sanctuary, cherubs were in the Most Holy Place above the mercy seat and the ark of the covenant with the Decalogue) became Satan, who began to destroy the peace, harmony, and joy in heaven. His pride, and selfishness ruined what was good, meaningful, and beautiful. As the archenemy of God, he brought chaos and disorder. He originated the great controversy on this earth when Adam and Eve broke their relationship with God and believed Satan's lies instead of trusting their loving Lord (Genesis 3:1–10). The intruder usurped rulership over the earth from Adam, which Jesus later regained by being our Representative as the Son of man and the Second Adam (Daniel 7:13, 14; John 12:31; 16:11; 1 Corinthians 15:22, 45). At the core of the great controversy are questions about God's person, understanding His actions, and believers' allegiance to Him and His law. The metanarrative of

Satan's rebellion against God gives important insight into the overall biblical-theological teaching (Job 1; 2; Isaiah 14:12–15; Ezekiel 28:11–19; Matthew 4:1–11; Luke 10:18; John 8:44; Revelation 12:4–17).[6] This spiritual warfare is also recognized by non-Adventist scholars[7] and has a cosmic dimension.[8] Thus, the great controversy is not just about the right day of worship, or worship itself, but the character of God and who He is. The Living God is the God of love, truth, and justice, and only such a God can be respected, loved, followed, and worshiped.

The Pentateuchal history

The five books of Moses present a long sweep of history. Beginning with Creation, when everything was in perfect harmony, they tell the story of the entrance of sin and humanity's struggles with evil, culminating with Israel's preparation to enter the Promised Land. This Pentateuchal narrative can be summarized in seven historical stages:

1. Early history narrative (from Creation to Abraham): Genesis 1–11
2. Patriarchal narrative (Abraham, Ishmael, Isaac, Esau, Jacob, and Joseph): Genesis 12–50
3. Egypt narrative (from Joseph to the ten plagues on the Egyptian gods and those who were associated with them): Exodus 1:1–12:30
4. Exodus narrative (the journey from Egypt to Sinai, almost a three-month period): Exodus 12:31–18:27
5. Sinai narrative (describes a nearly one-year stay at the mount of God): Exodus 19:1–Numbers 10:10
6. Wilderness narrative (thirty-eight years of wandering): Numbers 10:11–21:35
7. On the plains of Moab narrative (covers the last months of the life of Moses): Numbers 22–Deuteronomy 34

It is important to recognize that at the center of the Pentateuchal narrative is the story of the Exodus—the so-called Exodus narrative. The Exodus from Egypt is the event par excellence in the Old Testament (as well as in humankind's history), in which a people were spectacularly liberated from the dominion of another nation. To our best knowledge, this happened in 1450 BC and demonstrates how God miraculously delivered Israel from Egypt with His mighty hand. He opened the Red Sea to give them freedom and thus performed one of the most outstanding miracles in history. This grand intervention by God was a model of how God planned to lead His people to the Promised Land: The people would not have to fight any battles. The Lord would fight for them and give them a new place to live (Exodus 14:13, 14).

It is interesting that the early history narrated in the first eleven chapters of the book of Genesis describes a long period involving several millennia—from Creation until Abraham, who was born either in 2170 BC according to the Masoretic text (counted using the long chronology) or 1955 BC (counted according to the short chronology). The next historical period, the patriarchal narrative, mentions events from Abraham to Joseph, covering approximately the next three hundred years. The Egypt narrative describes historical activities that encompass events from the death of Joseph, the enslavement of Israel, and the birth and call of Moses, to the ten plagues in Egypt (Exodus 1–12), spanning more than two hundred additional years. The central Exodus narrative is a very significant but short period of time, about two months in length (Exodus 12–18)—with the Exodus occurring in 1450 BC.[9] The Sinai narrative describes events of nearly a year (Exodus 19:1; Numbers 10:11–13); however, this one year occupies the longest part of the Pentateuch, revealing Moses' focus on this period (Exodus 19–Numbers 10:10). The following wilderness narrative describes Israel's wandering in the wilderness for thirty-eight years. The final historical part of the Pentateuchal narrative is related to Israel's stay on the plains of Moab and depicts the last year of Moses' life as leader of Israel.

The biography of Moses

The book of Deuteronomy is the closing biography of Moses, who was a model leader and prophet of Israel. It is the culmination of what was previously described in the books of Exodus, Leviticus, and Numbers and presents events from the last two months of Moses' life. His last words are remarkable, and through Deuteronomy, he intends to renew the covenant between Israel and God, preparing his people to live in the new Promised Land.

The book of Deuteronomy is the story of how God patiently works with people, using Moses to help them walk on the right path. This story begins with the Israelites camping on the plains of Moab, ready to enter Canaan. For forty years, Moses has led them, but he will not lead them into their new home. Instead, he delivers three passionate speeches to Israel. In these speeches, he addresses the most important things the people of God need to know and observe when they enter the new territory. The narrative of the book continues with the explanation of legislation that is needed in the Promised Land. It progresses with the renewal of the covenant, the leadership change, the song of Moses, and his blessings on the Israelite tribes. It concludes with the death of Moses. Though the story covers a portion of Moses' life and the experience of God's people, the narrative is primarily about God and how He cares for His people. In his sermons, Moses reviews God's leading in Israel's history, expounding upon His laws, love, and faithfulness. After the death of Moses, the book of Joshua picks up the story and tells of the conquest and distribution of the Promised Land.

The glorious history of God's leadership is stunning. Israel witnesses His dramatic providence in the ten plagues, the Exodus from Egypt, the defeat of mighty Pharaoh and his army, crossing the Red Sea, and the gift of the Decalogue at Sinai. God is clearly the Lord who intervenes in our history, mingling His mercy with judgment. He proves that He is the God of love, truth, and justice, giving us the confidence to face an uncertain tomorrow.

1. Ellen G. White, *Life Sketches of Ellen G. White* (Mountain View, CA: Pacific Press®, 1943), 196. See also Ellen G. White, *Testimonies to Ministers and Gospel Workers* (Mountain View, CA: Pacific Press®, 1962), 31.

2. Ellen G. White, *The Ministry of Healing* (Mountain View, CA: Pacific Press®, 1905), 479.

3. The name of the book of Deuteronomy is derived from the Greek word *deuteronomion* (a composition of two words: *deuteros* and *nomos*), which means "second law" or "repetition of the law" as it occurs in the Septuagint, but it is an inaccurate translation of the Hebrew phrase *mishneh hatorah*, signifying a "copy of the book" or a "copy of the law" (Deuteronomy 17:18). This misleading title gives the impression that the book is about the law, and Moses is a lawgiver. Thus, these claims are confusing. In the Hebrew canon, the book carries the title *elleh hadevarim*—"These Are the Words"—according to the first two words of the biblical text.

4. See especially the five volumes of the Conflict of the Ages series by Ellen G. White: *Patriarchs and Prophets* (Oakland, CA: Pacific Press®, 1890); *Prophets and Kings* (Mountain View, CA: Pacific Press®, 1917); *The Desire of Ages* (Oakland, CA: Pacific Press®, 1898); *The Acts of Apostles* (Mountain View, CA: Pacific Press®, 1911); and *The Great Controversy* (Mountain View, CA: Pacific Press®, 1911). See also John C. Peckham, *The Love of God: A Canonical Model* (Downers Grove, IL: InterVarsity, 2015).

5. José M. Bertoluci, "The Son of the Morning and the Guardian Cherub in the Context of the Controversy Between Good and Evil" (ThD diss., Andrews University, 1985).

6. White, *Patriarchs and Prophets*, 34–44; White, introduction to *The Great Controversy*, v–xii; Jiří Moskala, "Origin of Sin and Salvation According to Genesis 3: A Theology of Sin," in *Salvation: Contours of Adventist Soteriology*, ed. Martin F. Hanna, Darius W. Jankiewicz, and John W. Reeve (Berrien Springs, MI: Andrews University Press, 2018), 119–143; Richard M. Davidson, "Satan's Celestial Slander," *Perspective Digest* 1, no. 1 (1996): 31–34; Jiří Moskala, "The God of Job and Our Adversary," *Journal of the Adventist Theological Society* 15, no. 2 (Autumn 2004): 104–117.

7. Gregory A. Boyd, *God at War: The Bible and Spiritual Conflict* (Downers Grove, IL: InterVarsity, 1997); Michael S. Heiser, *The Unseen Realm: Recovering the Supernatural Worldview of the Bible* (Bellingham, WA: Lexham Press, 2015).

8. See Jiří Moskala, "The Significance, Meaning, and Role of Christ's Atonement," in *God's Character and the Last Generation*, ed. Jiří Moskala and John C. Peckham (Nampa, ID: Pacific Press®, 2018), 190–218.

9. For details, see *The Seventh-day Adventist Bible Commentary*, vol. 1, rev. ed. (Washington, DC: Review and Herald®, 1976), 182–196; William H. Shea, "Exodus, Date of the," in *The International Standard Bible Encyclopedia*, vol. 2, rev. ed., ed. Geoffrey W. Bromiley et al. (Grand Rapids, MI: Eerdmans, 1982), 230–238.

CHAPTER

Two

Moses' History Lesson

The God of Moses led His people in a mighty yet gracious way for forty years. As Israel pauses on the brink of entering the Promised Land, Moses preaches his first sermon, urging Israel to reflect on God's actions, follow His leading, and trust His promises (Deuteronomy 1–4). He presents a clear and attractive picture of God in his speech, describing God's leadership in a meaningful way. The God of Moses is a God of relationships, a God who enters into close fellowship with Israel. Moses' Lord is a God of love, mercy, and forgiveness. He is a personal God. Moses repeatedly describes Him as "the LORD *our* God" and "the LORD *your* God." The theological exposition of the deity is centered on these phrases, and they occur more frequently in Deuteronomy than in any other book of Holy Scripture.

Two key phrases

The deity's name *LORD* (Yahweh) and the term *God* (Elohim) appear for the first time at the beginning of the first speech: "The LORD our God spoke to us in Horeb" (Deuteronomy 1:6a, NKJV). God spoke to Israel at Horeb, which is Mount Sinai. (Sinai is consistently called Horeb in Deuteronomy [1:2, 6, 19; 4:10, 15; 5:2; 9:8; 18:16; 29:1] with one exception in Deuteronomy 33:2.) It is remarkable how this extraordinary and majestic event influenced everything in the book of Deuteronomy. With His magnificent voice, God declared the Ten Commandments (Deuteronomy 4:10–15), which is the foundation of Moses' exposition of God's law in Deuteronomy.

The expression "the LORD our God" is found twenty-three times in Deuteronomy (Deuteronomy 1:6, 19, 20, 25, 41; 2:29, 33, 36, 37; 3:3; 4:7; 5:2, 24, 25, 27 [twice]; 6:4, 20, 24, 25; 29:15, 18, 29). But the whole book is permeated with another statement—the phrase "the LORD your God" is employed 280 times in different forms, singular and plural, with and without prepositions (Deuteronomy 1:10, 21, 26, 30, 31, 32; 2:7 [twice], 30; 3:18, 20, 21, 22; 4:2, 3, 4, 10, 19, 21, 23 [twice], 24, 25, 29, 30, 31, 34, 40; 5:6, 9, 11, 12, 14, 15 [twice], 16 [twice], 32, 33; etc.). These two expressions are the key declarations for God in the book of Deuteronomy. Their frequency underlines the fact that the book is Moses' passionate speech describing the covenant relationship between God and His people. These two confessional formulas appear in different forms more than three hundred times. No other biblical book contains such a concentrated frequency of these phrases or even comes close.

This statistical observation shines even more in comparison to the occurrences in other biblical books. While in the NKJV, the expression "the LORD your God" appears 280 times in the book of Deuteronomy, the same phrase is distributed in the rest of the Pentateuch in the following way: Genesis (onc time), Exodus (sixteen times), Leviticus (twenty-four times), and Numbers (four times). The closest books in terms of the frequency of the usage of this important relational expression outside of the Pentateuch are the following: Joshua (thirty-two times), 1 and 2 Chronicles (fifteen times), Jeremiah (fourteen times), 1 and 2 Samuel (thirteen times), 1 and 2 Kings (eleven times), Isaiah (nine times), Joel (seven times), Ezekiel (four times), and so on. After Deuteronomy, the most frequent usage of the phrase "the LORD our God" is in the book of Jeremiah, where it is employed seventeen times, and then in the Psalms, occurring ten times.

This is a stunning discovery. Moses focuses on these two phrases, which are consistently used in the first thirty-one chapters of Deuteronomy. Surprisingly, these key phrases are missing in the concluding chapters of the book (Deuteronomy 32–34). Why? First, chapters 32 and 33 are written in poetry, not in prose, and chapter 34 describes Moses' death in the third person. Second, at the climax of the book (Deuteronomy 32; 33), Moses' tone is very personal; he is singing and blesses the tribes of Israel. And third, he describes God in these final chapters with colorful vocabulary. For example, in his song in chapter 32, he uplifts the name of the Lord and praises the greatness and faithfulness of God, also stating that God is the Rock, the Father, the Creator, the Most High, and an Eagle. He masterfully portrays the Lord as the Sovereign Judge and compassionate Priest who makes "atonement for His land and His people" (verse 43, NKJV). Nowhere else in the book of Deuteronomy is a cluster of God's epithets mentioned with such richness and intensity.

Thus, these two expressions—"the LORD our God" and "the LORD your God"—serve as golden threads throughout the book. They are present in all three sermons of Moses (Deuteronomy 1:6–4:43; 4:44–28:68; 29:1–30:20), linking the entire book together. They also point to a close relationship between the Lord and Israel. The Lord is the personal God of His people: He is Yahweh and Elohim; He is transcendent yet also their immanent and close God; He is the God of the covenant. These two dimensions of Israel's Deity are emphasized, but the weight of their meaning is on the personal, intimate connection between God and His people. Moses stresses that the Lord is "your" and "our" God. These confessional formulas identify the Lord and His relationship to His people.

Additionally, it is important to realize that the self-recognition phrase "I am the LORD your God" occurs in two key places in the document. The first occurrence is within the Decalogue (Deuteronomy

5:6, 9), and the second is when Moses makes his ultimate appeal for Israel to follow God faithfully (Deuteronomy 29:6, NKJV).

The theme and seven crucial reminders of recent history

The principal theme of the book of Deuteronomy can be summarized in the following words: *Choose life—love, obey, and fear the Lord.* Deuteronomy's message is about our awesome Lord and how to respond to His love, care, and holiness.

After the introduction (Deuteronomy 1:1–6a), which presents the historical and situational background of the book, Moses begins his first powerful address to Israel (Deuteronomy 1:6b–4:43). He reminds the people how God has led them in the recent past while in the wilderness. His starting point is their one-year stay by the mountain of God. The new Israelite generation entering the Promised Land needs to be reminded of how God has been leading them and what He has done for them. So Moses chooses to present a series of seven crucial reminders—seven characteristic stories from the time of the pilgrimage from Horeb (Mount Sinai) to the brink of the Promised Land. These stories teach the people how God has cared for them (Deuteronomy 1:6b–3:29), and Moses follows the reminders with an exhortation to be faithful to the Lord (Deuteronomy 4:1–40). Here are the seven significant retrospective points:

1. *God's promise and the appointment of leaders at Horeb (Deuteronomy 1:6b–18).* The first thing Moses recalls for Israel is God's promise to give the special land to Abraham and his descendants. God had given His word, so they were secure in their hope for the future. Yet the Israelites had to wait more than four centuries for this to happen (Genesis 15:13–16), and because of their unbelief and rebellion, they were delayed another thirty-eight years (Deuteronomy 2:14). But God kept His word as He had announced to Abraham (Genesis 12:1, 7; 15:18–21), Isaac (Genesis 26:2–4), and Jacob (Genesis 35:11, 12), leading to this moment when they would enter the Promised Land. This clear promise of the land was an integral part of God's blessing to

Abraham and his posterity. The Israelites could now go forward courageously because God was with them.

Like Israel, it is easy for modern believers to feel that the fulfillment of God's promise has been delayed. But God always delivers on His Word, even when He is not in sync with our timetables and wishes. He does what He says He will do, and following Him means patiently waiting for the fulfillment of His promises, according to His timing and His plans. And eventually, step by step, the plan becomes clear. As a wise man once said, a journey of a thousand miles begins with a single step.

In Israel, leaders were appointed to be responsible for making sure all of God's guidelines were followed according to His will. These leaders were wise, knowledgeable, and respected individuals who were to judge the people impartially and without fear, knowing that "judgment belongs to God" (Deuteronomy 1:17, NIV). This was a tremendous help for Moses' administrative burdens.

2. *Journey from Mount Horeb to Kadesh, sending the spies, and the rebellion against the Lord at Kadesh (Deuteronomy 1:19–46).* After more than a year of camping at Mount Sinai (Exodus 19:1; Numbers 10:11), God encouraged Moses and the people of Israel to move forward and enter the land of Canaan. Unfortunately, on the brink of entering Kadesh, the people rebelled against God (Numbers 14). This serious disobedience was of such a deep character that the trust relationship between the people and God was broken. It happened after twelve spies reported what they had seen and experienced in the new territory (Numbers 13). Ten of them gave a discouraging message that led to Israel's disobedience (verses 27–33). This terrible rebellion against God and Moses changed Israel's destiny. Because of a lack of trust in God, the Exodus generation lost their opportunity to enter the Promised Land.

3. *Wandering in the wilderness around the hill country of Seir and the Transjordan—Israel commanded not to fight with Edom, Moab, and Ammon (Deuteronomy 2:1–23).* God, as their Leader, continued to

guide His people through their wandering in the wilderness. In spite of their rebellion and unfaithfulness, the Lord was gracious to Israel and took care of their daily needs, so they "lacked nothing" (verse 7). The Lord commanded Moses to bypass Edom, Moab, and Ammon because of their close family relationship with Israel. God did not allow Israel to fight those countries because He gave them their territories, and they were protected by Him.

4. *Victory over Sihon, king of Heshbon—the conquest of the Transjordan (Deuteronomy 2:24–37).* The Lord graciously and tangibly demonstrated that He was with His people by giving them victory over the powerful King Sihon from Heshbon in the Transjordan. This victory was a sign assuring the people that He would lead them to inherit the Promised Land and that they should trust God to open the way for them to enter Canaan.

5. *Victory over Og, king of Bashan—the conquest of the Transjordan (Deuteronomy 3:1–11).* God, in His mercy, gave Israel a second victory—this time over Og, king of Bashan—thus confirming that the victory over Sihon did not happen by chance. As Og and Sihon were defeated, so other kings would be defeated, and Israel would possess the land. It was the beginning of their triumphant conquest because God as the Mighty Warrior fought for them and gave them this victory (verse 3). This was a concrete assurance that Israel would continue to systematically conquer the Promised Land, being delivered from their enemies as God had promised.

6. *Distribution of the land to the two and a half Transjordan tribes and the command to them (Deuteronomy 3:12–20).* The Transjordan territory conquered by Israel was given to two and a half tribes of Israel—namely, the Reubenites, the Gadites, and the half tribe of Manasseh. It was their place to live and prosper. For the other tribes, this distribution of the land was a visible foretaste that they would also receive their portions of land in the near future. The two and a half Transjordan tribes, however, had to send their warriors to assist the other tribes in conquering the land of Canaan. But the Israelites

had to realize that God is the Owner of everything (Psalm 24:1, 2), and the land Israel was to possess was His precious gift and blessing to them in order for them to flourish.

7. *Moses' encouragement to Joshua to conquer the land, and his plea with the Lord to enter the Promised Land (Deuteronomy 3:21–29).* God instructed Moses that Joshua, not him, would lead Israel into the Promised Land. Unfortunately, Moses had not completely trusted God and failed to honor Him and uplift His holiness before Israel (Numbers 20:2–12). As a result, Moses was not allowed to enter the earthly Canaan. It is evident that Moses is burdened with his failure from his three "complaints" in his first sermon (Deuteronomy 1:37; 3:26; 4:21). He knew that he would soon die (Deuteronomy 3:27), but his deep desire was to go with God's people and experience the fulfillment of God's promise to Abraham.

In spite of his deep dissatisfaction and disappointment, Moses is not bitter. He encourages Joshua, his servant, and appoints him as the new leader, ready and willing to courageously conquer Canaan. Joshua assumes this leadership role, and the book of Joshua testifies that he faithfully fulfills the enormous task of leading the Israelites into their new home.

After these seven historical reminders, Moses, in the culmination of his first sermon, closes with an appeal to Israel to follow God, exhorting the people to obey and trust the Lord because of the practical and beneficial consequences for them (Deuteronomy 4:1–40).

Personal application

As you review and evaluate your personal life, take a moment to recognize the following crucial events: when God called you to Himself, touched you with His love, intervened on your behalf, protected you, surprised you with His tender care, sent people to your aid, or stopped you from doing wrong things. You will likely recognize many critical points in your life.

The time you spend evaluating the past is important for two reasons.

First, it is crucial in times of difficulty and uncertainty to remember that God has always led His people. You, your family, and even an institution can rest assured that God will not abandon His people in the present situation. This realization encourages confidence for the future. Second, it is particularly vital to remember God's leading during tough times, when you are standing at a crossroads, wondering what to do, and agonizing over a difficult decision that needs to be made. At this juncture, taking a moment to recognize God's leading in the past will bring calm and confidence to the present. You can march forward through the labyrinth of life, following the path that God has already trodden.

CHAPTER

Three

The Everlasting Covenant

God loves humanity with "an everlasting love" (Jeremiah 31:3) and made an everlasting covenant with His people (Jeremiah 32:40; Ezekiel 37:26; Hebrews 13:20). The covenant that He initiated and renewed with Israel (Exodus 19:4–6; 24:3–7), He reaffirms through Moses in the book of Deuteronomy. He does this because He wants to deepen, renew, and seal the covenant between His people and Himself, encouraging them to be faithful to Him through all of life's circumstances in the Promised Land.

The book of Deuteronomy is written in a complex literary structure (for details, see the appendix at the end of this book). I was pleasantly surprised to discover that the whole document is presented in the form of a covenant. I was even more amazed to learn that three structures are mingled together in the book. This is extremely significant because I do not know of any other biblical book where three literary structures play key roles within the same volume.

First, a rhetorical structure unites Moses' three speeches or discourses (Deuteronomy 1:6–4:43; 4:44–28:68; 29:1–30:20).[1] Second, the covenant structure binds together the entire book in six parts: the preamble (Deuteronomy 1:1–6a), historical prologue

(Deuteronomy 1:6b–4:43), stipulations (Deuteronomy 4:44–26:19), blessings and curses (Deuteronomy 27:1–30:20), witnesses (Deuteronomy 30:19; 31:19), and special provisions of the covenant (Deuteronomy 31:9–13).[2] Finally, the exposition of each of the Decalogue's commandments is presented in the central part of the book in the second sermon. This is achieved as follows: first, the law's principles are clarified in chapters 5–11, and then each commandment is explained in chapters 12–26.[3] This threefold literary structure adds to the beauty of the text, underlines Moses' intentionality, and helps the reader to perceive the book's big picture. Furthermore, the unity of the book is validated by these structures, making it evident that one mastermind, guided by the Holy Spirit (2 Timothy 3:16; 2 Peter 1:20, 21), is behind this outstanding composition.

The making of a covenant

What is a *covenant*? The best answer to this fundamental question is quite simple: it is a document outlining the motif of a close bond, contract, or treaty that binds two parties together. Because the trust relationship between God and His people had been marred, God initiated a covenantal step by putting this relationship of two unequal parties into written form. Deuteronomy was a legal document containing the features, conditions, and specifics of a meaningful relationship, how it was to work and then was to be cut (ratified) with His people.

A written agreement must be established when there is mistrust between two parties who need to do something together. For example, if I wish to buy a car from my colleague, and I trust him because I know that he is a person of integrity, we do not need to engage in complicated paperwork. I trust him, and he trusts me; because of the trustworthiness of our words, we have enough confidence to proceed with a simple transaction between us. But if I do not trust my colleague, or he has doubts about my ability to pay him on time, we would need to protect this transaction with a written agreement. Lack of trust demands an official legal procedure to establish a strong contract. The less trust there is, the more a safeguard is needed. These precautions ensure the security of the relationship.

When God's people do not cultivate a trust relationship with Him, He graciously establishes a covenant with them to assure them that He is for them, He is always faithful and trustworthy, and He keeps His word. What a beautiful God who longs for a meaningful relationship with His followers. He takes the first step to restore the brokenness (as He did in the Garden of Eden when Adam and Eve sinned against Him [Genesis 3:9]). Thus, this God of relationships establishes a covenant with His people.

The first explicit appearance of the word *covenant* occurs in Genesis 6:18 when God promises Noah that He will enter into a covenant with him and his family in order to save a faithful remnant (Genesis 7:23). After the Flood, God makes His covenant with the whole world: Noah, his descendants, and every living thing on the earth (Genesis 8:21, 22; 9:8–17). This Noahic, post-Flood covenant is unilateral, and God Himself states what He will do, regardless of humanity's response: He will faithfully keep His promise and never again destroy the earth by a flood. The rainbow is the visible sign of God's unconditional faithfulness—a promise to keep His word (Genesis 9:13–17).

In the Adamic covenant, God declares that He will send the Promised Seed to redeem fallen humanity (Genesis 3:15; Matthew 1:21). His Word guarantees its fulfillment because what God vows He delivers (Psalm 33:6, 9). In the fullness of time, God sends Jesus Christ into the world to save us (Daniel 9:24–27; John 3:16; Galatians 4:4). He is always committed to us and does everything possible to persuade humanity to follow Him, for He is for us and never against us (Romans 8:31–39).

In the Abrahamic covenant, God Himself reassures Abraham that He will be cut into pieces like sacrificial animals if He breaks the covenant with him (Genesis 15:7–19).[4] Wow! God came to Abraham with fire and smoke, pointing to His presence as in Exodus 19:18, and "passed" (Hebrew *'abar*) between the pieces of the animal sacrifices, pledging that His promise of the land to Abraham's descendants will stand (Genesis 15:17, NKJV). *Passing through* was a significant concept, and the term was also used at the time of the Exodus, when the Lord passed through (*'abar*) Egypt to strike the Egyptians who were not covered by the blood of the Passover lamb (Exodus 12:12, 21–23). Not long after that event, Israel triumphantly passed through (*'abar*) the Red Sea (Exodus 14:21; Psalm 66:6).

An important aspect of God's covenant with Abraham is that it was not a bilateral agreement—a covenant between two parties. On the contrary, it depended solely upon God's action. God would do what He promised in spite of Israel's hesitance to believe Him. J. Nicholas Reid aptly states, "In Genesis 15 the Lord is taking all the obligations on himself. May he be cursed; may he die if the covenant is violated. As the New Testament teaches, the unthinkable happened at Calvary, when God was cursed and died for his people (Acts 20:28)."[5]

There are not many covenants in the Old Testament, but there is only one eternal covenant of grace or peace. This covenant has seven different phases or forms in history: Adamic covenant (Genesis 1–3), Noahic covenant (Genesis 6–9), Abrahamic covenant (Genesis 12:1–3; 15:1–21; 17:1–27), Mosaic or Sinaitic covenant (Exodus 19–24), Phinehas covenant (Numbers 25:10–13), Davidic covenant (2 Samuel 7:5–16), and the new covenant (Jeremiah 31:31–33).[6]

The structure of the Mosaic covenant and some of the other biblical covenants are built on the pattern of Hittite suzerainty-vassal treaties, which were also used in Egypt.[7] To communicate in a meaningful way, God used a method that Israel could understand, and Moses communicated the message of God's faithfulness to His covenant in this well-recognized pattern.[8]

Assyriologist Viktor Korošec published a study of his findings on the treaties between Hittite kings and their vassals. In his analysis, he discovered several well-defined, distinct parts that had quite a regular sequence.[9] Then George Mendenhall of the University of Michigan compared Korošec's study with biblical covenants.[10] As a result, Bible scholars were surprised to realize that a similar pattern was used in describing God's establishment of covenants with His people. What a stunning discovery!

How were the ancient covenants of Moses' time put together? The structures were built on the Hittite suzerainty-vassal treaties' pattern, so parts of the biblical covenants were similar:

1. Preamble (the Lord presents Himself; who He is)
2. Historical prologue (the past relationship between the Lord and His people is explained)
3. Stipulations (commands are formulated; obedience is stimulated)
4. Blessings and curses (those who obey will receive blessings; the disobedient receive curses)
5. Witnesses (witnesses can be people, the earth, heaven)
6. Sign of the covenant and/or special provisions (rainbow, circumcision, reading of the law on special occasions, monuments, etc.)

The following are examples of such structures:

1. *The Decalogue (Exodus 20:1–17).* Though it only reflects a part of this form, the Decalogue does demonstrate how the form works: preamble (verse 2a), historical prologue (verse 2b), stipulations (verses 3–17), witnesses (verses 18–21), blessings and curses (Leviticus 27), and special provisions (Deuteronomy 6:6–9).
2. *The book of Deuteronomy.* Deuteronomy has a preamble (1:1–6a), historical prologue (1:6b–4:43), stipulations (4:44–26:19), blessings and curses (27:1–30:20), witnesses (30:19, 20), and special provision (31:9–13).
3. *Joshua 24.* The Lord renews the covenant with Joshua: preamble

> (Joshua 24:2a), historical prologue (verses 2b–13), stipulations (verses 14, 15, 23), blessings and curses (verses 19, 20), witnesses (verse 22), and special provision (verses 25–27).

A careful study comparing the covenants of the first and second millennia BC with Deuteronomy leads to the significant conclusion that the covenant structure in the book of Deuteronomy reflects the second millennium BC Hittite vassal treaties. Paul Lawrence pointedly states, "So by way of a summary: It can be concluded that the form of the pentateuchal covenants has much more in common with the Second Millennium BC treaties than with their counterparts from the First Millennium BC. This suggests that the pentateuchal covenants are Second Millennium BC in their origin."[11] He further underlines this: "It is striking that Historical Prologues do not occur in the Aramaic and Neo-Assyrian treaties of the First Millennium"[12] and that "there are no blessings in the First Millennium Assyrian treaties."[13]

While it is true that the form of the literary structure of the biblical covenants is taken from the Hittites, it should also be remembered that the content is new. A closer examination of Moses' writing reveals that this biblical covenant is a work of genius! The activity of the Holy Spirit is behind it; the means are worldly, but the message is divine.

The purpose of the message is to effectively communicate the truth about God and His faithfulness to His people. Furthermore, He clearly tells His people how they should respond and live in a close relationship with Him. The renewal covenant is full of God's warm affection and demonstrates His longing for a close relationship with His people—a longing that was manifested in the life and death of our Lord Jesus Christ.

---

1. "Preliminary results from a consideration of the vocabulary of Deuteronomy, show that 699 of the 1,285 individual words identifiable in the book can be found in non-Hebrew texts

from the third and second millennia (54.4 per cent of the whole), whereas only 97 words can be found exclusively in first millennium non-Hebrew texts (7.5 percent). 454 examples (35.4 per cent) of the vocabulary of Deuteronomy have no parallels outside of the Hebrew material, and 35 (2.7 percent) require further investigation." Paul Lawrence, *The Books of Moses Revisited* (Eugene, OR: Wipf & Stock, 2011), 12n47.

2. Outstanding covenant studies include the following publications: William W. Hallo and K. Lawson Younger Jr., eds., *The Context of Scripture*, 4 vols. (Leiden: Brill, 2003); Kenneth A. Kitchen, *Ancient Orient and Old Testament* (Chicago, IL: InterVarsity, 1966), 90–102; Kenneth A. Kitchen and Paul J. N. Lawrence, *Treaty Law and Covenant in the Ancient Near East*, 3 vols. (Wiesbaden: Harrassowitz Verlag, 2012); Meredith G. Kline, *Treaty of the Great King: The Covenant Structure of Deuteronomy: Studies and Commentary* (Grand Rapids, MI: Eerdmans, 1963); Lawrence, *Books of Moses Revisited*; Skip MacCarty, *In Granite or Ingrained? What the Old and New Covenants Reveal About the Gospel, the Law, and the Sabbath* (Berrien Springs, MI: Andrews University Press, 2007); Dennis J. McCarthy, *Old Testament Covenant: A Survey of Current Opinions* (Atlanta, GA: John Knox, 1972); Dennis J. McCarthy, *Treaty and Covenant*, Analecta Biblica 21a (Rome: Pontifical Biblical Institute Press, 1981); Steven L. McKenzie, *Covenant*, Understanding Biblical Themes (St. Louis, MO: Chalice Press, 2000); George E. Mendenhall, "Covenant Forms in Israelite Tradition," *Biblical Archaeologist* 17, no. 3 (September 1954): 50–76; O. Palmer Robertson, *The Christ of the Covenants* (Phillipsburg, NJ: Presbyterian and Reformed, 1980); John H. Walton, *Covenant: God's Purpose, God's Plan* (Grand Rapids, MI: Zondervan, 1994); and Gordon J. Wenham, *Exploring the Old Testament*, vol. 1, *The Pentateuch* (London: SPCK, 2003), 123–143.

3. The elaborate Decalogue structure of the book of Deuteronomy was introduced by W. Schultz, *Das Deuteronomium* (Berlin: Gustav Schlawitz, 1859) and improved by Stephen A. Kaufman, "The Structure of the Deuteronomic Law," *MAARAV* 1, no. 2 (Spring 1979): 105–158. It is now accepted and followed by many scholars, such as Mark E. Biddle, *Deuteronomy*, Smyth & Helwys Bible Commentary (Macon, GA: Smyth & Helwys, 2003), 197–203; Andrew E. Hill and John H. Walton, *A Survey of the Old Testament*, 2nd ed. (Grand Rapids, MI: Zondervan, 2000), 131–143; Walter C. Kaiser Jr., *Toward Old Testament Ethics* (Grand Rapids, MI: Zondervan, 1983), 127–137; Eugene H. Merrill, *Deuteronomy: An Exegetical and Theological Exposition of the Holy Scripture*, New American Commentary (Nashville, TN: B&H Pub., 1994), 218; Dennis T. Olson, *Deuteronomy and the Death of Moses: A Theological Reading* (Minneapolis, MN: Fortress, 1994); Edward J. Woods, *Deuteronomy*, Tyndale Old Testament Commentaries (Downers Grove, IL: IVP Academic, 2011), 49–55.

4. For details, see Gerhard F. Hasel, "The Meaning of the Animal Rite in Genesis 15," *Journal for the Study of the Old Testament* 6, no. 19 (February 1981): 61–78; Jacques B. Doukhan, *Genesis*, Seventh-day Adventist International Bible Commentary (Nampa, ID: Pacific Press®, 2016), 222–228.

5. J. Nicholas Reid, "Ancient Near Eastern Backgrounds to Covenants," in *Covenant Theology: Biblical, Theological, and Historical Perspectives*, ed. Guy Prentiss Waters, J. Nicholas Reid, and John R. Muether (Wheaton, IL: Crossway, 2020), 465.

6. See MacCarty, *In Granite or Ingrained?*; Gerhard F. Hasel, *Covenant in Blood* (Mountain View, CA: Pacific Press®, 1982).

7. For details, see Lawrence, *Books of Moses Revisited*, 47–64; McCarthy, *Old Testament Covenant*, 10–22; and Woods, *Deuteronomy*, 37–47.

8. For Egyptian and Hittite influences on the concept and structure of the covenant, see

James K. Hoffmeier, *Ancient Israel in Sinai* (New York: Oxford University Press, 2011), esp. 181–192. Lawrence correctly underlines, "The pentateuchal covenants, although essentially following the late Second Millennium treaty form, were not its slavish imitators," *Books of Moses Revisited*, 62.

9. Viktor Korošec, *Hethitische Staatsverträge: ein Beitrag zu ihrer juristischen Wertung* (Leipzig: T. Weicher, 1931).

10. George E. Mendenhall, *Law and Covenant in Israel and the Ancient Near East* (Pittsburgh, PA: Presbyterian Board of Colportage of Western Pennsylvania, 1955).

11. Lawrence, *Books of Moses Revisited*, 64.

12. Lawrence, 69.

13. Lawrence, 76.

CHAPTER

Four

To Love the Lord Your God

Moses reveals God's passionate love for Israel in the closing chapters of Deuteronomy. Using poetic language and colorful imagery to describe the Lord, he sings a song and offers a blessing over the children of God. Deuteronomy 32 and 33 contain astonishingly rich imagery about God. He is the Creator, Father, Rock, Eagle, Savior, King, Shield, Refuge, Sword, and Helper. He is great, eternal, faithful, upright, and jealous. He does no wrong. He loves, puts to death, brings to life, avenges, makes atonement, liberates, guides, protects, legislates, and provides for the needs of people. He reveals, watches, guards, and blesses. Moses also stresses God's uniqueness (Deuteronomy 32:39; 33:26). God is everything to His people. He is for them and never against them. To make sure everyone understands what he is saying about God, Moses makes this final proclamation:

> Blessed are you, Israel!
> Who is like you,
> a people saved by the LORD?
> He is your shield and helper
> and your glorious sword (Deuteronomy 33:29, NIV).

God's compelling love

Because the Lord of Israel loves so affectionately and tenderly, God's people are drawn to respond to Him. His love motivates them and from the fountain of God's goodness springs a response of gratitude. Only when people experience and appreciate God's unselfish love are they able to love. John expresses this thought clearly when he says, "We love Him because He first loved us" (1 John 4:19, NKJV).

In the plan of salvation, the announcement of the good news of the gospel comes first. It is the indicative (pronouncement of fact) of God's love. It is followed by the imperative of the gospel—what we need to do. This proper sequence of applying God's truth in our lives is crucial. Initially, the gospel is proclaimed—salvation in Jesus Christ our Lord—then it is followed by the commands of the gospel. First comes grace and then obedience, first is faith and then work, and first is the experience of salvation and then the law is internalized and obeyed. Grace accepted through faith is the root of salvation, and ethics is its fruit and result. We were created and redeemed by our gracious Lord, and the recognition and appreciation that He is our Creator and Savior leads us to also accept Him as our Lord and King. The more we know of and experience His goodness, the more we are open to His power to change our lives, liberate us from our slavery to sin, and enable us to follow and worship Him. In our complex world, He leads us in our decisions and actions so we will reflect His values. For example, God brings the children of Israel out of Egypt, gives them freedom, and only then does He give them the gift of the Decalogue. The apostle Paul explains this magnificent truth of genuine conversion to the believers in Rome: "Do you despise the riches of His goodness, forbearance, and longsuffering, not knowing that the goodness of God leads you to repentance?" (Romans 2:4, NKJV).

There are numerous examples of this truth. At Creation, God makes everything perfect. After making humans the crown of His creation, He commands Adam and Eve to follow His instructions in order to live happy and satisfactory lives. He wants them to keep the Garden of Eden, His perfect gift for them, in its original perfect state (Genesis 1:28–31; 2:15–17). When Adam and Eve sin and hide from God, the Lord, in His grace, searches for them: "Where are you?" (Genesis 3:9). This action became the pattern of redemption. God always takes the first step and is the Initiator of our salvation (Philippians 2:12, 13).

In his Epistle to the Romans, Paul explains the gospel like this: we are all sinners without exception and need Jesus Christ as our Savior (Romans 1–8). He applies these foundational truths to the Jewish nation (chapters 9–11) and then highlights the consequences of these facts—namely, how the redeemed in Christ ought to live (chapters 12–16). Paul aptly states, "Therefore, I urge you, brothers and sisters, in view of God's mercy, to offer your bodies as a living sacrifice, holy and pleasing to God—this is your true and proper worship. Do not conform to the pattern of this world, but be transformed by the renewing of your mind. Then you will be able to test and approve what God's will is—his good, pleasing and perfect will" (Romans 12:1, 2, NIV). The apostle does the same in the Epistle to the Ephesians: he first speaks about the riches of God's mercy (Ephesians 1–3) and then points out how to walk in the light of the gospel (chapters 4–6). This is an important pattern: we need to proclaim God's grace first and then help those who are touched by His love to know how to follow Him in the power of His Spirit (Romans 8:1–17).

Moses strongly exhorts believers to love God because the only proper response to the God of love is to love Him. Ten times the author calls Israel to love God (Deuteronomy 6:5; 10:12; 11:1, 13, 22; 13:3; 19:9; 30:6, 16, 20) and underlines that God blesses those who love Him (Deuteronomy 5:10; 7:9). Believers also need to love people by loving the aliens among them because God loves them too (Deuteronomy 10:18, 19). The book also expresses a servant's love for his master (Deuteronomy 15:16) and a husband's love for his wife (Deuteronomy 21:15, 16). Deuteronomy is God's love letter to His people, and Moses eloquently paints God's affection, faithfulness, and passion for

His children in his speeches. Deuteronomy centers on God's love for Israel, which demands a total commitment to love in return. The love of God is presented as the primary motivation for obedience. Thus, Deuteronomy reminds all of God's true followers that they, as a community of believers, are called to remember the love of the Lord and put into practice their love for the Lord by obeying His law and showing love toward others. God loves us; therefore, we must love!

What is *love*?

The command to love may cause us to pause and wonder whether love can be ordered. Two of the greatest commands in Scripture begin with the imperative to love God: love Him with all your heart, and love your neighbor as you love yourself (Leviticus 19:18; Deuteronomy 6:5; Matthew 22:37–40; Luke 10:27). It is shocking to learn that God demands and orders us to love. How is this possible? How can love be commanded? Postmodern people are confused about the nature of love because of its portrayal by Hollywood and mass media. The misguided message about love goes like this: Love is something personal and private. While love is a nice feeling, our feelings can change; they are vulnerable to the circumstances of life. If it feels good, it must be good and right.

But does true love depend on our feelings, which are unstable, insecure, and misleading? On the other hand, how can affection be commanded? In response to such important questions, we need to realize that, in the biblical sense, good feelings follow love and doing the right things. Love is not defined by feelings or an occasional high experience.

True love, contrary to popular opinion, goes beyond our present emotions, sentiments, or passions. First, biblical love is a decision, much like marital love is a decision for life (Genesis 2:24). Second, genuine love is a commitment. Faithfulness plays a crucial role in it. In that sense, the real question before marrying someone is not whether we love that person but whether we are committed to that person, no matter what happens. We can only learn about genuine love from the real love abundantly manifested in the life of Jesus. Christ loved us even when we were sinners and at enmity with Him (Romans 5:6–8; Ephesians 2:1–3, 12). This leads to the third point: love is a principle. It is not shaped by current emotions. We decide, commit, and follow. It is more than an emotional attitude or rational calculation; it is total involvement. From an attitude of wholehearted commitment flows joy, peace, harmony, happiness, collaboration, security, and stability. This is why God reveals that love is a command, a principle, and a solid foundation on which everything else depends.

Someone wisely stated that love is a verb because love is always in action and focuses on others, not self. In the New Testament, the best definition of true love is provided by the apostle Paul in 1 Corinthians:

> Love is patient, love is kind. It does not envy, it does not boast, it is not proud. It does not dishonor others, it is not self-seeking, it is not easily angered, it keeps no record of wrongs. Love does not delight in evil but rejoices with the truth. It always protects, always trusts, always hopes, always perseveres.
>
> Love never fails. But where there are prophecies, they will cease; where there are tongues, they will be stilled; where there is knowledge, it will pass away (1 Corinthians 13:4–8, NIV).

Love is above all, and by this type of genuine love, every action is judged. This is why Paul can state, "If I speak in the tongues of men or of angels, but do not have love, I am only a resounding gong or a clanging cymbal. If I have the gift of prophecy and can fathom all mysteries and all knowledge, and if I have a faith that can move mountains, but do not have love, I am nothing. If I give all I possess to the poor and give over my body to hardship that I may boast, but do not have love, I gain nothing" (verses 1–3, NIV).

Thus, the modern myth of sentimental love is defeated. Emotionalism is nice for a moment, but in long-term commitments, it does not help and may even be harmful by causing pain, disappointment, and depression. Love is a fragile flower of heavenly origin that needs to be constantly cultivated and watered so it does not fade or disappear. It would be profitable for each of us to learn 1 Corinthians 13 by heart, meditate on it daily, and put it into practice. Through the power of the Holy Spirit, all of our relationships would be improved.

Learn to fear God

Love is closely connected with fearing God. In modern languages, this association has been lost because the semantics of *fear* and *love* do not link these two concepts. We associate fear with negative emotions and attitudes, such as being afraid of a person or a situation. But in the Bible, fearing God is tied to loving Him and being totally dedicated to Him as lovers are committed to each other. One of the best texts to prove this is Deuteronomy 10:12, in which Moses states, "And now, Israel, what does the LORD your God require of you, but to fear the LORD your God, to walk in all His ways and to love Him, to serve the LORD your God with all your heart and with all your soul" (NKJV). The text explains by appositions what it means to fear God: it means to walk in all of His ways—that is, to obey Him, love Him, serve Him completely, be at His disposal, and be His channel of blessing to others.

Fearing God is a vital and highly prominent teaching that appears in key places within Deuteronomy. Study carefully Deuteronomy 4:10; 5:29; 6:2, 13, 24; 8:6; 10:12, 20; 13:4; 14:23; 17:19; 25:18; 28:58; 31:12, 13.[1] The idea of fearing the Lord occurs fifteen times in Deuteronomy. Overall, there are twenty-three uses of the Hebrew word *yare'* ("fear," "afraid," "terrible," "reverence") in Deuteronomy without the connection to the fear of God (out of thirty-eight total occurrences of the word), such as in Deuteronomy 1:19, 21, 29; 2:4; 7:19; 11:25; 28:10.[2] The Lord is an "awesome God" (Deuteronomy 7:21; 10:17), and the people of God need to learn how to fear Him by following the teachings and directions in Deuteronomy.

Fearing God means deciding to follow Him and His teaching in every moment of life. It means living in His presence, being aware of Him, and making decisions in regard to Him and His will. It is significant that Moses underlines several times that we do not know how to fear God or how to love and obey Him; we need to learn how to do these things (Deuteronomy 14:23; 31:12, 13). Even future kings needed to carefully study the book of Deuteronomy in order to learn to fear the Lord (Deuteronomy 17:19). Before God, we are like small children who need to learn how to walk with Him.

What does it mean to fear God?

No command of God is given in a vacuum. The requirement to fear God presupposes a knowledge of God's goodness and His character of love. The Lord is faithful, kind, merciful, holy, and just. These qualities and virtues attract us to God because He is full of compassion, grace, patience, and forgiveness, and He is always in search of His lost children. God Himself reveals these characteristics to Moses: "The LORD, the LORD, the compassionate and gracious God, slow to anger, abounding in love and faithfulness, maintaining love to thousands, and forgiving wickedness, rebellion and sin. Yet he does not leave the guilty unpunished" (Exodus 34:6, 7, NIV). This self-revelation by God is the foundational message of who He is. It is like a precious diamond with brilliant facets or like a golden thread woven into a tapestry. It is the John 3:16 of the Old Testament and permeates God's revelation, often being repeated or paraphrased in key places within the Holy Scriptures (e.g., Numbers 14:18; Nehemiah 9:17; Psalms 86:15; 103:8; 145:8; Joel 2:13; Jonah 4:2).

This observation teaches us that we can only fear God if we appreciate Him and His attributes. Only when we are grateful for what He has done and what He is doing in our lives will the fear of God become more than a concept. Only then will it become a lifestyle, not just an additional activity in our performance but a joyful life in God's presence, lived according to His regulations. It is our response to experiencing God's grace and leadership in our lives that completely transforms the way we think and feel. It influences our goals, our plans, and everything we do.

In simple terms, what does it mean to fear God? It means cultivating God's presence in our hearts and making decisions within the setting of His grace, thus respecting Him, His revealed will, and His objectives for us. God's presence purifies our thinking and motives, causing us to delight in the Lord and in His law (Psalms 1:2; 37:4; Proverbs 3:5, 6). In this way, we learn how to trust Him and grow in Him.

Therefore, respect and reverence toward God lie behind this short bidding, which has such immense implications. To fear God is to be on His frequency and hear His voice's leading. No wonder fearing God is the first imperative of the everlasting gospel (Revelation 14:6, 7). It changes everything in our lives because His presence in us is everything.[3]

---

1. Jiří Moskala, "The Meaning of the Fear of God: The Crucial Notion of the Everlasting Gospel–a Biblical Study," *Journal of the Adventist Theological Society* 30, nos. 1, 2 (2019):1–20.
2. The noun "fear" occurs once (Deuteronomy 2:25), and the adjective "fearful" is employed once (Deuteronomy 20:8).
3. Jiří Moskala, "The Indispensable God's Presence: Toward the Theology of God's Face," *Current* 8 (Fall 2020): 36–43.

CHAPTER

Five

The Stranger in Your Gates

The phrase "The Stranger in Your Gates," the title of this chapter, is a reference to the fourth commandment: "The seventh day is the Sabbath of the Lord your God. In it you shall do no work: you, nor your son, nor your daughter, nor your male servant, nor your female servant, nor your ox, nor your donkey, nor any of your cattle, nor your stranger who is within your gates, that your male servant and your female servant may rest as well as you" (Deuteronomy 5:14, NKJV). The Israelites were to be kind to strangers and foreigners because they were to remember that they had been slaves in Egypt, and God had liberated them. He mercifully gave them freedom from that bondage: "And remember that you were a slave in the land of Egypt, and the Lord your God brought you out from there by a mighty hand and by an outstretched arm" (verse 15, NKJV).

In Deuteronomy 10:19, Moses similarly states: "Therefore love the stranger, for you were strangers in the land of Egypt" (NKJV). The Israelites were admonished to be kind to immigrants and remember that they had been foreigners in Egypt. It was not a time for revenge but for compassion and kindness. Their acts of mercy would demonstrate their appreciation for God's merciful work on their behalf.

Since they were now free, in their prosperity, they should always think about others in need by helping them in meaningful ways. God advised the Israelites not to treat strangers as they had been treated in Egypt. They needed to esteem everyone and grant them respect. Foreigners or strangers were to have the right to prosperous lives. Being strangers in Egypt, they knew the bitterness and humiliation of that experience, so they were to treat foreigners with compassion, dignity, care, and love. No one was to be mistreated, starved, or made poor. Strangers were to be included in the experience of Sabbath rest.

Abraham was also a stranger, a foreigner, and an immigrant in the land of Canaan (Genesis 23:4; compare Hebrews 11:9). God blessed him because he demonstrated unselfishness toward others (Genesis 14:22–24; 18:1–8). The author of Hebrews, having in mind the episode of Abraham entertaining the three visitors, declares: "Do not forget to show hospitality to strangers, for by so doing some people have shown hospitality to angels without knowing it" (Hebrews 13:2, NIV). The Israelites were taught to assist people facing difficult times: "If any of your fellow Israelites become poor and are unable to support themselves among you, help them as you would a foreigner and stranger, so they can continue to live among you" (Leviticus 25:35, NIV).

Social justice

The principle of social justice demands that we value each other highly because we were all created by God in His image (Genesis 1:27). There is no exception. Even though sin has marred this image in a dramatic way, we should treat each other with respect because the one who diminishes God's creatures disrespects the Creator.

Both the Pentateuch and the Old Testament prophets underline the importance of providing practical help to strangers. This help goes hand in hand with care for the poor, fatherless, and widowed (Exodus 22:21–27; Leviticus 23:22; Deuteronomy 10:18; 14:29; 16:11, 14; 24:17–21; 26:12, 13; 27:19; compare Psalms 9:8, 9; 10:18; 68:5, 6;

82:3; 146:7, 9). The biblical prophets are extremely eloquent on this issue. Consider these five Old Testament prophetic statements.

1. Isaiah admonishes, "Learn to do right; seek justice. Defend the oppressed. Take up the cause of the fatherless; plead the case of the widow" (Isaiah 1:17, NIV; compare Isaiah 10:1–3; 58:6, 7).
2. Jeremiah cries out, "Do justice and righteousness, and deliver from the hand of the oppressor him who has been robbed. And do no wrong or violence to the resident alien, the fatherless, and the widow, nor shed innocent blood in this place" (Jeremiah 22:3, ESV; compare Jeremiah 22:13, 16; Ezekiel 22:7).
3. The prophet Amos admonishes, "But let justice roll on like a river, righteousness like a never-failing stream!" (Amos 5:24, NIV).
4. The prophet Zechariah powerfully declares, "Thus says the LORD of hosts, Render true judgments, show kindness and mercy to one another, do not oppress the widow, the fatherless, the sojourner, or the poor, and let none of you devise evil against another in your heart" (Zechariah 7:9, 10, ESV; compare Jeremiah 21:12).
5. The prophet Malachi writes down the Lord's statement: "So I will come to put you on trial. I will be quick to testify against sorcerers, adulterers and perjurers, against those who defraud laborers of their wages, who oppress the widows and the fatherless, and deprive the foreigners among you of justice, but do not fear me" (Malachi 3:5, NIV).

"For I, the LORD, love justice" (Isaiah 61:8, NIV; compare Jeremiah 9:24). Love and justice must always go together (Hosea 12:6; compare Hosea 2:19). In the New Testament, James stresses the same theme: "Religion that is pure and undefiled before God the Father is this: to visit orphans and widows in their affliction, and to keep oneself unstained from the world" (James 1:27, ESV; compare James 2:2–6).

The two greatest commandments—loving God and loving your neighbor—are inseparable (Mark 12:28–31). You cannot love God and hate your brother or sister or a foreigner or a stranger. John uses extremely strong language to make the point clear: "Whoever claims to love God yet hates a brother or sister is a liar" (1 John 4:20, NIV).

In order to live an unselfish, God-centered, and neighbor-centered life, we need to let God transform us. In the words of Moses: "Circumcise your hearts" (Deuteronomy 10:16, NIV). This command is uttered in the setting of Israel's stubbornness: "Do not be stiff-necked any longer" (verse 16, NIV). It is not enough to be outwardly circumcised. What is needed is a new heart (Ezekiel 11:19), and this transformation cannot be achieved by human effort. Transplantation of the heart is only possible by God's special intervention in our lives. It is the Spirit of God who performs the miracle of replacing the "heart of stone" with "a new heart" (Ezekiel 36:26, NIV). Ezekiel calls the new heart "a heart of flesh" (verse 26, NIV), meaning a heart that is sensitive, thoughtful, compassionate, and obedient.

God's Sabbath commandments should help us in this regard. The Sabbath demonstrates that we are deeply valued, embraced, and loved by the God who created and redeemed us. The dignity of all people is underlined in the Sabbath commandment, revealing the inherent worth of every human being, regardless of age, gender, education, race, nationality, social status, religion, or achievement. We are created in God's image, and no one can take this asset from us. God's plan is to restore His image to its fullness by the transforming power of His grace, His Word, and His Spirit. This kind of relationship with God can be meaningfully cultivated on the Sabbath. He has given us this gift, this "palace in time,"[1] so we can worship our High Priest and King. The delightful fellowship and exquisite communion with our Creator, Redeemer, King, Priest, and Prophet should lead us to become friends with Jesus (as Moses was [Exodus 33:11]) and lovingly serve the people around us (Luke 10:36, 37; John 13:34, 35).

Reflections on the Sabbath and social justice

It is significant that the idea of caring for a stranger and servants as well as animals is articulated in the Sabbath commandment. It is expressed in a specific context that should be carefully studied because the fourth commandment is often seen from a narrow perspective—namely, as a day of rest from work, as a day for worship in the church, or as a part of the important controversy between keeping the Sabbath versus observing Sunday. Though these aspects of the commandment are important, they form only a part of its rich meaning. The social aspect of this commandment should not be overlooked. Kindnesses to strangers, slaves, and animals are major concerns and integral parts of the Sabbath commandment. This also means that environmental and social studies have roots in this legislation as well as in the biblical account of Creation (Genesis 1; 2).

Many sincere students of the Bible are puzzled and even shocked by the realization that the Bible contains two biblical versions of the Sabbath commandment, and they slightly differ from each other. It is interesting that the Decalogue written in Exodus 20 is dissimilar to the one in Deuteronomy 5, mainly in regard to the Sabbath commandment. They ask, How can this be? Did not God write the commandments on the two tablets? So how can they differ? The two versions of the Sabbath commandment mainly diverge in the motivation clause. These two accounts are giving dissimilar reasons for keeping the Sabbath holy. Let us briefly compare these two accounts.

Two versions of the Sabbath commandment

The Exodus version goes like this:

> "Remember the Sabbath day, to keep it holy. Six days you shall labor and do all your work, but the seventh day is the Sabbath of the Lord your God. In it you shall do no work: you, nor your son, nor your daughter, nor your male servant, nor your female servant, nor your cattle, nor your stranger who is within your

gates. For in six days the LORD made the heavens and the earth, the sea, and all that is in them, and rested the seventh day. Therefore the LORD blessed the Sabbath day and hallowed it" (Exodus 20:8–11, NKJV).

The Deuteronomy version is slightly different:

"Observe the Sabbath day, to keep it holy, as the LORD your God commanded you. Six days you shall labor and do all your work, but the seventh day is the Sabbath of the LORD your God. In it you shall do no work: you, nor your son, nor your daughter, nor your male servant, nor your female servant, nor your ox, nor your donkey, nor any of your cattle, nor your stranger who is within your gates, that your male servant and your female servant may rest as well as you. And remember that you were a slave in the land of Egypt, and the LORD your God brought you out from there by a mighty hand and by an outstretched arm; therefore the LORD your God commanded you to keep the Sabbath day" (Deuteronomy 5:12–15, NKJV).

These two Sabbath accounts have the same principal thoughts: God's followers need to keep the Sabbath day holy, and they should work six days but not work on the seventh day. When comparing these two records, we perceive the following modifications:

1. The first words differ: Exodus 20:8 employs the verb "Remember" (Hebrew *zakar*), used in the sense of not forgetting the Sabbath day and keeping it fresh in the mind and heart. Deuteronomy 5:12 uses the verb "Observe" (Hebrew *shamar*), meaning to keep, take care of, and live the Sabbath day.
2. Deuteronomy 5:12 includes an additional clause—"as the LORD your God commanded you"—which can be understood as an emphasis stressing its divine origin.

3. Deuteronomy 5:14 contains the extra words "nor your ox, nor your donkey, nor any of [your cattle]," thus expanding rest to the animal world and stressing its inclusivity.
4. The same verse has a further elaboration on the rest of the servants: they "may rest as well as you," which underlines the equality of rest for the different members of the household.
5. The major difference is in the motivational phrase for the day of rest on the Sabbath. Exodus 20 provides the six-day Creation as the reason: "For in six days the LORD made the heavens and the earth, the sea, and all that is in them, and rested the seventh day. Therefore the LORD blessed the Sabbath day and hallowed it" (verse 11). Deuteronomy 5 explains this Sabbath obligation from the perspective of the deliverance from Egypt: "And remember that you were a slave in the land of Egypt, and the LORD your God brought you out from there by a mighty hand and by an outstretched arm; therefore the LORD your God commanded you to keep the Sabbath day" (verse 15).

How should we understand these differences, especially the different rationales? The reason for the differences lies in the simple fact that these two versions were issued on two separate occasions when the historical reality had changed. In Exodus, God Himself proclaims the Ten Commandments on Mount Sinai (Exodus 20:2–17), and then He inscribes them onto two stone tablets and gives them to Moses in that written form (Exodus 31:18; 32:19; 34:4, 28; 40:20). But in Deuteronomy 5, Moses recites the Sabbath commandment in his sermon, and he applies the content to the Israelites' liberation from the bondage of slavery and their new social situation without denying the Creation reason for the Sabbath's observance. He just does not mention or comment on it. So the difference is in the rhetoric of Moses, who is preaching to Israel and applying this commandment to his audience and their recent Exodus experience. As an inspired prophet (Deuteronomy 18:15), he correctly interprets the intention of this commandment because the situation demands it. He faithfully expands on the purpose of the commandment by explicitly noting the different enumerated entities—servants, strangers, and animals. The previous text of the covenant code puts the social aspect in the forefront: "Six days you shall do your work, and on the seventh day you shall rest, that your ox and your donkey may rest, and the son of your female servant and the stranger may be refreshed" (Exodus 23:12, NKJV).

In Exodus 20, the Sabbath is rooted in Creation, and in Deuteronomy 5, its social dimension is highlighted—namely, the deliverance and freedom of the oppressed. Moses is delineating the theology behind the Sabbath, highlighting the redemptive and social aspects of the fourth precept for all in addition to the Creation motif. Thus, these two Sabbath rationales are complementary and help us to understand the Sabbath commandment from a broader perspective.

In Deuteronomy, the Sabbath commandment is connected to the first two commandments that preclude having other gods or making any idols. According to these two commandments, only the Lord can be the Master and Organizer of our social lives. Thus, the Sabbath reminds people that they are created in the image of God. There is no exception; all are God's children: men, women, children, servants, slaves, and foreigners. The Sabbath liberates people from social barriers and prejudices. It calls for humans to be kind and caring, not only to those around them but also to strangers, marginalized individuals, and even animals. No discrimination is possible if the Sabbath is truly kept because discrimination is based on distinctions of sex, color, social status, education, nationality, or religion. All are created equal. Moses emphasizes that God is a personal God and that each human being is a unique person and should be treated with respect and dignity.

Various types of social designations are reiterated in Deuteronomy 5 to clarify the social order. Nine groups are enumerated: you (your spouse is implicitly included), your son, your daughter, your male servant, your female servant, your ox, your donkey, your cattle, and the stranger. Care for the animal world points to ecological concerns, echoing the phrase that the Lord created "the heavens, the earth, the sea, and everything in them" (Exodus 20:11). As human beings, we should protect God's created order, just as Adam and Eve were commissioned to do at Creation (Genesis 1:26, 28).

During His ministry, Jesus also stresses caring for people in need. Four times in His parable about the last judgment (Matthew 25:31–46), He enumerates six activities, including loving-kindness for strangers, always in the same sequence: "I was hungry and you gave me something to eat, I was thirsty and you gave me something to drink, I was a stranger and you invited me in, I needed clothes and you clothed me, I was sick and you looked after me, I was in prison and you came to visit me" (verses 35, 36, NIV). The individuals in the parable automatically act unselfishly, as though this is their life's normal routine and practice, so they are surprised when they hear a high acclamation from the King Himself: "Whatever you did for one of the least of these brothers and sisters of mine, you did for me" (verse 40, NIV).

Acts of mercy only have value when they are performed from pure motives of love, compassion, and kindness (1 Corinthians 13:1–3). The prophet Micah eloquently summarizes this biblical ethic with these familiar words:

> He has shown you, O mortal, what is good.
> And what does the LORD require of you?
> To act justly and to love mercy
> and to walk humbly with your God (Micah 6:8, NIV; compare Deuteronomy 16:20).

1. Abraham J. Heschel, *The Sabbath: Its Meaning for Modern Man* (New York: Farrar, Straus and Giroux, 2005), 15.

CHAPTER

Six

For What Nation Is There so Great?

The phrase "what other nation is so great" is a quotation from Deuteronomy 4:7, NIV. In Deuteronomy 4, God explains to His people why they are different and the conditions on which they may retain their greatness. The reason for their uniqueness lies in God—their Leader. The core of the matter is that their Lord is a living God, great, holy, gracious, wise, just, and full of understanding. This is why His people can also be great, wise, and understanding. Their distinctiveness is anchored in (1) God's presence with them, (2) God answering their prayers, and (3) God giving them wise and just laws (Deuteronomy 4:6–8).

After Moses reminds Israel how God graciously and miraculously has led them for nearly forty years—from Egypt to the plains of Moab and now to the border of the Promised Land—he exhorts them to be faithful to the Lord. He points to seven key events during their journey from Mount Sinai (Deuteronomy 1–3) and admonishes God's people to listen and follow their mighty God and not the "man-made gods of wood and stone, which cannot see or hear or eat or smell" (Deuteronomy 4:28, NIV). These idols are nothing, but Israel's God proves to be a loving Lord.

After the history lesson, in Deuteronomy 4, Moses explains the purpose of the first sermon. Israel's future prosperity depends on respecting God, His Torah, and His instructions. This principle is aptly captured in the last two verses of Moses' speech: "Acknowledge and take to heart this day that the LORD is God in heaven above and on the earth below. There is no other. Keep his decrees and commands, which I am giving you today, so that it may go well with you and your children after you and that you may live long in the land the LORD your God gives you for all time" (verses 39, 40, NIV).

In his speech, Moses leads the people to consider important principles of life in order to remain a godly and unique nation. Deuteronomy 4 can be divided into the following five sections:

1. *The Holy God gives the law and judges His people (Deuteronomy 4:1–8).* Moses begins his plea with the key word "hear" (Hebrew *shama'*), meaning to listen or obey. People need to hear God's instructions and then obey them, which is a frequent theme in Deuteronomy (Deuteronomy 4:1; 5:1; 6:4; 9:1; 20:3) because the Lord's blessings flow from a deep relationship with the Him and obedience to Him and His law. When someone is willing to hear and pay close attention to God's law (the Israelites were not deaf), it means that the person understands the issues of life and does what is right, thus following God's divine instructions and voice (Deuteronomy 4:30; 6:3; 12:28; 27:10; 30:2, 8). Those who hear and understand God's Word will love, keep, and obey it. This is a natural outcome of knowing God's goodness. Such people will follow Him out of gratitude, not because they have to but because they want to. The Lord's kindness leads people to repentance and thankfulness, and their appreciation of His faithfulness prompts them to be faithful, creating in them the best motives.

The Lord has given the Israelites the Torah and is now giving them the land. They will retain their home and their country permanently on the condition that they live in harmony with God's revealed will.

The principles of His law are unchangeable and normative, so they cannot alter His commands (Deuteronomy 4:2). They need to keep them and live according to their original intent.

The people of God need to take the God of Moses seriously because to follow Him and His teaching is a matter of life and death. Moses explains this issue with two examples: (1) the tragic events at Baal Peor (verse 3, NIV), as described in Numbers 25, where people disregarded God's directions and died; and (2) his own failure to follow God's directions, as revealed in Numbers 20 (Deuteronomy 4:21). No one is exempt from obedience and God's judgment. Those who hold "fast to the Lord"—even better, those who *cling* (Hebrew root *dabaq*; see Genesis 2:24; Ruth 1:14) to Him like a husband to his beloved wife—pass positively through His judgment and maintain life (Deuteronomy 4:4; compare Deuteronomy 10:20). To enjoy the fullness of life and its happiness, God has given them wise and just laws; if they are obeyed, other nations will admire the Israelites as an esteemed nation.

2. *The sovereign God speaks and initiates the covenant (Deuteronomy 4:9–14).* Since the Lord spoke out of the fire at Horeb, this motif is mentioned several times, always in connection with theophany (verses 12, 15, 33, 36). God is a "consuming fire" (verse 24, NKJV) because He is the Judge. He has established the covenant with Israel, and this fact is mentioned three times in this chapter (verses 13, 23, 31), showing that this is a dominant topic. Making a covenant is God's way of demonstrating His initiative, faithfulness, and the permanence of His connection and fellowship with people. God's Word, as expressed in the Ten Commandments, is the core of this covenant (verse 13).

3. *God's covenant in a nutshell: warning against idolatry (Deuteronomy 4:15–24).* Moses, in the central passage of his appeal, warns Israel against idolatry. When God had spoken to them at Horeb, they did not see His form; thus, they cannot put the infinite and eternal God into any material representation, such as a carving,

picture, statue, or figurine. Instead, people need to cultivate a relationship with the Living God on a spiritual level. According to verse 20, God has saved, rescued, and claimed them as His special possession and now commands them to keep His laws and refrain from making idols.

4. *The merciful God calls for witnesses and faithfulness (Deuteronomy 4:25–31).* The title of the conclusion of Moses' first sermon (Deuteronomy 4:1–40) can be captured in a sentence borrowed from the book of Hebrews: "Seeing Him who is invisible" (Hebrews 11:27, NKJV). God never reveals Himself to Israel in any specific form but speaks to them only by voice: "You heard the sound of words but saw no form; there was only a voice" (Deuteronomy 4:12, NIV; see also Deuteronomy 4:15, 33, 36; 5:5, 22–26). This is why He is not to be confined to any image or sculpture, making Him into an idol. He transcends all human categories of imagination. He is a living God, so no form can capture who He is. Israel's only duty is to gratefully follow His guidance and obey His teaching.

5. *The loving God and the final appeal for obedience (Deuteronomy 4:32–40).* The Lord of Israel is an extraordinary, awesome, and magnificent God. In Deuteronomy 4, He is presented as "the LORD" (verses 1, 3, 12, 14, 15, 20, 21, 27, 35, 39), the "God of your fathers" (verse 1, NKJV), the "LORD your God" (verses 2, 3, 4, 10, 19, 21, 23 [twice], 24, 25, 29, 30, 31, 34, 40), the "LORD my God" (verse 5), the "LORD our God" (verse 7), a "consuming fire" (verse 24, NKJV), a "jealous God" (verse 24), "God" (verses 32, 33, 35), "His Presence" (verse 37, NKJV), and "God in heaven above and on the earth beneath" (verse 39, NKJV). God reveals Himself to His people as an active Lord who intervenes in human affairs "by signs and wonders, by war, by a mighty hand and an outstretched arm, or by great and awesome deeds" (verse 34, NIV). He loves the Israelites (verse 37), and this is why He chose them, brought them out of Egypt in a spectacular way, and gave them His laws. Moses begs them to obey God's instructions and teachings because obedience is crucial for a successful future.

God's gift of the Torah

How is it possible that Israel became so great as a nation? As explained above, Moses' answer is threefold (verses 6–8), but the main reason was the fact that God gave them wise and great laws. The Decalogue was the Magna Carta of everything, and all the other laws sprang from the Ten Commandments. This is Moses' principal theme in his second sermon (Deuteronomy 4:44–28:68), where each law, precept, decree, command, stipulation, and statute (different synonymous terms point to the specific corpus of the distinct laws; see Deuteronomy 4:1, 5, 14, 40, 44; 5:1; 6:1, 2, 20, 24; 7:9, 11; 8:11; 11:1; etc.) is carefully explained as an extension of the Decalogue.

Some of the other ancient Middle Eastern collections of laws that precede the time of Moses are similar, but the majority of Israel's legislation is unique to Israel. The Code of Hammurabi, written around 1750 BC (three hundred years before the Exodus), with its 282 laws, is not the first surviving code of law. It is predated by the Code of Ur-Nammu (from approximately 2100 BC), the Code of Lipit-Ishtar (circa 1930 BC), and the Laws of Eshnunna (from around 1770 BC).[1] These collections of laws from Mesopotamia are the most well known, but no extrabiblical law collections contain legislation that is similar or close to the Decalogue. The Ten Commandments stand high above all other legislation. The book of Deuteronomy expounds on the Torah (Deuteronomy 1:5), and the Pentateuchal laws contain ethical, moral, and social regulations as well as cultic legislation that can be summarized in seven main codes:

1. The Decalogue (Exodus 20:2–17; Deuteronomy 5:6–21)
2. The covenant or social code (Exodus 20:22–23:33)
3. The ritual code (Exodus 34:10–26)
4. The sacrificial code (Leviticus 1–7)
5. The purity code (Leviticus 11–15)
6. The holiness code (Leviticus 17–26)
7. The Deuteronomic code (Deuteronomy 12:1–26:19)

As is clear from this overview, all of these biblical codes follow the foundational constitution of the Ten Commandments.

The Deuteronomic law has a detailed connection to the Decalogue and depends on it, as Stephen A. Kaufman convincingly demonstrates and aptly concludes with this emphatic note in his study on the structure of the law in Deuteronomy: "The efforts of a century of scholarship to propose elaborate redactional histories for DL [Deuteronomic law] must be deemed fruitless. DL did not grow in stages as these scholars would have us believe. It is rather a unified masterpiece of jurisprudential literature created by a single author . . . into a highly patterned whole—an expanded Decalogue."[2]

The Decalogue is summarized and explained in the book of Deuteronomy in the following way:

1. The principles of God's law (chapters 5–11)
2. The first and second commandments: Worship (12:1–31)
3. The third commandment: Name of God (13:1–14:29)
4. The fourth commandment: Sabbath (15:1–16:17)
5. The fifth commandment: Authority (16:18–18:22)
6. The sixth commandment: Homicide (19:1–22:8)
7. The seventh commandment: Adultery (22:9–23:18)
8. The eighth commandment: Theft (23:19–24:7)
9. The ninth commandment: False charges (24:8–25:4)
10. The tenth commandment: Coveting (25:5–26:15)
11. Appeal to renew the covenant (26:16–19)

God's law is connected with wisdom, and wisdom is the ability to discern between good and evil and follow what is right. The Torah teaches this wisdom that will bring satisfaction and happiness into one's life. Wisdom, with its profound benefits from observing God's law, is excellently explained in Proverbs 3 and Psalms 1; 19; and 119.

Consider Psalm 19, which has two well-defined parts. In the first section, general revelation in nature is described (Psalm 19:1–6), but then David explains the splendor of God's special revelation in His law (verses 7–14). He uses six synonymous words to describe divine teaching. He speaks about the "law of the LORD," His "statutes," "precepts," "commands," "fear," and "decrees" (verses 7–9, NIV). Then he goes through sixteen different qualities and effects of the Lord's instruction: it is "perfect, reviving the soul," "trustworthy, making wise the simple," "right, bringing joy to the heart," radiant, giving light to the eyes, "pure, lasting forever," sure, altogether righteous, more precious than gold, "sweeter than honey," "warning," and giving "great reward" (verses 7–11). These values are immensely important and need to be experienced in life!

Greatness never appears in a vacuum. It goes hand in hand with incredible character and is associated with the virtues described in the Beatitudes and the qualities enumerated as the fruit of the Spirit. These virtues are usually not appreciated by the world because the natural heart admires power, strength, fame, heroism, and strong words. On the other hand, God teaches that greatness is found in humility, as taught by the Incarnation. Supposed greatness is connected with pride, selfishness, and the assumption that we can decide and do what we want. But true wisdom is always oriented toward the needs of others. We are not living to be happy but to make others happy. Thus, true greatness is associated with discipline, law, and order as well as sacrifice, service, compassion, and kindness.

Deuteronomy 4:6 mentions that the nations will admire the wisdom and understanding of the laws and decrees of Israel because they will see how God's people behave prudently. Through their observations, they will then understand the wisdom and greatness of Israel's Lord. The benefits of obedience will set Israel apart from other nations. The purpose for this greatness is so the Israelites "will be a blessing" to all people and nations—"all the families on earth" (Genesis 12:2, 3; compare Isaiah 49:6; Revelation 14:6). By their obedience to God, their good deeds will make Israel the salt and the light of the whole world (Matthew 5:13–16).

This obedience is possible because God is able to give us victory over temptation (1 Corinthians 10:13) and keep us from falling (Jude 24). The God of Moses is "a merciful God; he will not abandon or destroy you" (Deuteronomy 4:31). He is for us, and He proved it by giving us Jesus Christ as our Savior (John 3:16). Moses assures us: "If . . . you seek the LORD your God, you will find him if you seek him with all your heart and with all your soul" (Deuteronomy 4:29, NIV; compare Joel 2:12, 13).

1. Martha T. Roth, *Law Collections From Mesopotamia and Asia Minor*, 2nd ed., ed. Piotr Michalowski (Atlanta, GA: Scholars Press; Atlanta, GA: Society of Biblical Literature, 1997).

2. Stephen A. Kaufman, "The Structure of the Deuteronomic Law," *MAARAV* 1, no. 2 (Spring 1979): 147.

CHAPTER

Seven

Law and Grace

Many students of the Bible wonder about the proper relationship between the law and grace. *Grace* is rightly defined as "undeserved merit"—a free gift from God to save sinners. What we do not deserve, God is giving to us. His divine assistance to help us in our helplessness amazes us. What we cannot do for ourselves, He does unselfishly for us. Does this grace of God nullify His law? Of course not. Just as amnesty for a murderer does not abolish the law "You shall not murder" (Deuteronomy 5:17, NIV), so God's grace does not negate the law. Paul assures us: "Do we, then, nullify the law by this faith? Not at all! Rather, we uphold the law" (Romans 3:31, NIV). And again, the apostle underlines this: "Circumcision is nothing and uncircumcision is nothing. Keeping God's commands is what counts" (1 Corinthians 7:19, NIV). In his letter to the Galatians, he stresses, "For in Christ Jesus neither circumcision nor uncircumcision has any value. The only thing that counts is faith expressing itself through love" (Galatians 5:6, NIV).

The gift of the law

God's law is an extremely precious commodity for securing the harmonious function of His government, the prosperity of the whole universe, and the good of all beings. It is also crucial for us. In many passages in the book of Deuteronomy, the Lord, the God of Israel, is presented as the Lawgiver (Deuteronomy 4:2, 5, 11–14; 5:1–6, 9, 22–33; 6:18; 9:11; 10:1–5; etc.), and the story of Moses receiving the Decalogue is recounted. Out of His love and mercy, God formulates the foundational principles of love with their vertical and horizontal dimensions. Love for God is the focal point of the first four commandments, and love for our neighbors is the focus of the following six commandments (Deuteronomy 5:6–21). Thus, the two greatest commandments of love are explained in the Decalogue (Deuteronomy 6:5; Leviticus 19:18). God gave these eternal laws to the Israelites to guide and regulate their lives for their own good and well-being (Hebrew *letob lak* [Deuteronomy 10:13]). It was not the genius of Moses that invented the Torah of God. The Decalogue was the special gift of God to humanity. Its principles were in effect from the Creation of the world and known in a nutshell before Sinai,[1] but God Himself chose to present the Decalogue to His people and humanity because these essential principles had been forgotten. They are important for life because they reflect, in a systematic way, the eternal God, His character, and His values.

The Lord, the God of Moses, is the Legislator, and His law is the expression of His character because a law reflects its originator's character. As God is, so is His law (Psalm 19:7–11; Romans 7:12). Two simple illustrations will suffice: Pharaoh's law to kill the Hebrew baby boys (Exodus 1:22) and Herod's command to murder all boys under the age of two (Matthew 2:16) speak volumes about the wicked and unstable characters of these two tyrants. If I had the legislative power to give one hundred thousand dollars of tuition money to every fifteen-year-old who desired an education, this law would clearly reveal that I treasure education and want to give equal opportunities to everyone who wishes to acquire knowledge.

Truly, as the Lawgiver, God's law reflects Him by giving us a better knowledge of who He is and a clearer understanding of the ultimate purpose of His law. Our God of love bases His legislation upon love. Interpreting the law without having an understanding of God's love results in legalism and pride. The real problem with legalism is that legalists are unable to see themselves as legalists and consider themselves to be reformers who are zealous for the truth. They believe they uplift God's law and true obedience. Legalism is a trap to make people think that they are honoring the law, but they destroy it by their cold attitudes and behaviors. Knowing the letter of God's commandments without knowing the Commander and His intentions makes the law deadly (2 Corinthians 3:6). The law is a precious gift for humanity, but it can hurt if it is interpreted without love and strictly applied. It can be like a sharp scalpel in the hands of someone who wants to perform an operation but has not studied anatomy and knows nothing about surgery. Only a person deeply convicted of his or her own sin understands the real need for mercy in view of the perfect law and the Holy Author of the law.

The structure of the Decalogue

The Decalogue has a transparent structure: the first four commandments describe how to respect God, and the fifth through tenth commandments clearly define how to respect people around us. The second part begins with respect for a most important relationship—namely, the relationship with our parents. From this foundation, all other relationships emanate. The last six commandments champion respect for life, marriage, family, sexual purity, property, and the reputations of people. They culminate with respect for ourselves in order that no evil or wicked desires will be found in our hearts.

At the center of the Ten Commandments is the Sabbath commandment, placed there as a seal that combines both vertical and horizontal relationships. (It was customary in ancient times to put a seal in the middle of a scroll.) The Sabbath commandment contains the name, title, territory, and activity of God. He is the Lord our God who created "the heavens and the earth, the sea, and all that is in them" (Exodus 20:11, NIV).

The Sabbath is truly the theological center of the Decalogue. The Sabbath leads to the worship of the Creator as well as taking care of all people in a household, including strangers and animals. It is unique legislation in its content and social aspects. Love for God is always transformed into love for the people around us. The Sabbath should help us cultivate meaningful relationships. Love toward God is not only reflected in our worship but also in our relationships with our neighbors. It is an all-inclusive legislation, reflecting God's grace in a par excellence way. *Before* Adam and Eve began working (they were created on Friday as God's last crowning act), they celebrated life with their Creator.

The wonder of God's grace

As Seventh-day Adventist Christians, we confess that we follow Christ and do His will, not in order to be saved but because we are saved. Faith is not our savior—the saving role belongs exclusively to Jesus Christ. Faith is the hand by which we receive God's grace; it is the means through which we accept His redemption. Even though we are saved by God's abundant mercy through faith alone, faith never stands alone. Thankfulness motivates all of our doings. Faith is the root, and works are the fruit; grace is the cause of our submission to the Lord, and because of grace, we obey Him and keep His law.[2]

God always makes the initial move. He takes the first step. He is the Source of all good things in our lives; He leads us to respond correctly to His desire to save everyone (Genesis 3:9; 1 Timothy 2:3, 4; James 1:17; 2 Peter 3:9). Prevenient[3] (initial or enabling) grace influences our hearts and minds and empowers our wills to respond positively to His gentle call to return to Him (Philippians 2:13; compare Ephesians 2:1–5) and repent when His Word is preached to us (Isaiah 45:22; Joel 2:12, 13; Mark 1:15; John 12:32; Acts 2:38; Romans 10:17). Prevenient grace leads us to accept God's saving grace. Repentance is not our work; it is the result of opening our hearts to God and having Him change our minds and thoughts through the influence of His Spirit and Word. The Greek word *anothen*, which is used in Christ's statement "unless one is born again he cannot see the kingdom of God" (John 3:3, ESV), means "again" or "from above" (verses 3–8). This theological concept is further expanded in John 1:12; Romans 12:1; 2; and 1 Thessalonians 2:13. When we accept God's Word and do not resist His Holy Spirit, then new life and spiritual revival occur within us. We begin to do things for Christ and others because we are compelled to do them by His enabling grace, Word, and Spirit (Ezekiel 36:25–28; 37:4–10, 14; Zechariah 4:6; Romans 8:11; James 1:18; 1 Peter 1:23). But even if we do good works, we have nothing to boast about (Jeremiah 9:23, 24; 1 Corinthians 1:29–31) because God has already prepared the works in advance in order for us to walk in them (see Ephesians 2:10, ESV). We experience justification as well as sanctification by God's grace through faith: The Holy Spirit empowers us to be different and act in harmony with His will. Christ is alive today, interceding for us as the only, great, and all-powerful Intercessor. He saves us completely and enables us to do His will (Romans 8:34; 12:1, 2; 1 Timothy 2:5; Titus 2:11–14; Hebrews 7:25). Thus, obedience is made possible for the redeemed who are strengthened by the Spirit.

Crucial functions of God's law

The standard, or criterion, for divine judgment is the Decalogue—God's law. As James observes: "So speak and so do as those who will be judged by the law of liberty" (James 2:12, NKJV; compare Ecclesiastes 12:13, 14). The Decalogue is an objective norm, personified in the life of Jesus, who was the only Person who lived in perfect harmony with the law's requirements (John 8:46; Romans 2:16; 8:3, 4; 1 Corinthians 1:30; 2 Corinthians 5:21; Galatians 3:13; Hebrews 4:15).

In this context, we need to reflect on the principal functions of God's moral law. The function of *the law is not to gain salvation through its observance*; instead, *the Decalogue reveals our sinfulness* before our

Holy God *and leads us to Christ* in order to be purified, changed, and sanctified. Thus, the law guides the believer to Jesus and, through His grace, to obedience.

There are not two ways to salvation—one through obedience to the law and the other through grace—only one. Salvation is possible *exclusively* through Christ Jesus (Acts 4:12; Romans 3:22–26; Ephesians 1:4–10; Philippians 2:10). The "new covenant" had already been made with Israel (Jeremiah 31:31–33; Ezekiel 36:25–29) and was a renewal of God's original covenantal intent. Moses stressed it in the famous and foundational passage that includes the greatest commandment to love God (Deuteronomy 6:5–7, NIV). Jesus also made it clear in the Sermon on the Mount of Beatitudes when He stressed the need to internalize God's law (Matthew 5:17–48).

The law of God is not annulled in the new covenant but rather is established when it is implanted in the hearts of believers (Jeremiah 31:33; Hebrews 8:10). John R. W. Stott expresses this eloquently in his book on the interpretation of the Sermon on the Mount. He correctly argues that Jesus is not confronting the Old Testament teaching but the rabbinic interpretation of the Old Testament of His time because He is contrasting His "true interpretation of the law and the scribal misinterpretations."[4] Justification by faith is solidly established in the Hebrew Scriptures (Genesis 15:6; Psalm 32:1, 2; Habakkuk 2:4), so the true New Testament teaching is not built on wrong Old Testament texts.[5]

The law leads to Christ

God's holy law reveals how sinful we are (Romans 3:20, 23), but the law is unable to cleanse us. In this sense, it leads us to Christ (Galatians 3:24), who gives us His purity and the robe of His righteousness (Romans 3:24; 5:1, 8–11; 8:1; 1 John 1:7, 9). Only God's grace, through the power of His Word and Spirit, enables people to follow Christ and obey Him. When God's commandments are received as God's promises, then the Christian experience is about

His action and not our achievement; it is about what He can do in us and through us when we let Him.[6] Ellen White explains, "All His biddings are enablings."[7] The Decalogue is not merely a prohibition; it is first a promise and then a permanent commandment that brings a joyful life.

The law in the new covenant is planted in the heart. Those who keep the Decalogue properly will not consider it a burden but will follow its promises with the right motives, obeying out of gratitude for what God did and is doing for them. Grace does not change the law—it changes our attitude toward it.

In the New Testament, Paul is against legalism, not against the law of God (Romans 7:9–12; compare Psalm 19:8–12). He is against the misuse of the law as well as against the transgression of God's law. Christ took upon Himself the curse and punishment of the law (Galatians 3:13, 14), so we are no longer under the condemnation of the law but under God's grace (Romans 6:14, 15). Jesus Christ is the goal and purpose of the law (Romans 10:4), not the end in the sense of the termination or cessation of its validity. He gives meaning to the law, and it follows that believers who love Him will embrace the law as normative for their lives.

---

1. See Jo Ann Davidson, "The Decalogue Predates Mount Sinai: Indicators From the Book of Genesis," *Journal of the Adventist Theological Society* 19, nos. 1, 2 (2008): 61–81.

2. Scholars and translators are puzzled about how they should translate Psalm 119:29b. The best interpretation is to treat "your law/teaching/instruction" as an apposition—that is, the explanation of God's grace: "Grant me the grace, your law." The New Jerusalem Bible renders this text in the following way: "Grant me the grace of your Law." The 1984 NIV translates it: "Be gracious to me through your law." The law contains grace; it is about God's grace. The law is God's promise and His beatitude (not our performance), and in this sense, God's grace of the law triumphs. Obedience is always the result of His power through His Word in our lives.

3. The English word *prevenient* is derived from the Latin *praevenire*, meaning "come before, preceding, anticipating, expectant."

4. John R. W. Stott, *Christian Counter-Culture: The Message of the Sermon on the Mount* (Leicester, UK: InterVarsity, 1978), 78, 79. John Stott asks an important question: "But with whom is Jesus contrasting himself?" His answer is profound: "Many commentators have main-

tained that in these paragraphs Jesus is setting himself against Moses. . . . Popular as this interpretation is, I do not hesitate to say that it is mistaken. It is more than mistaken; it is untenable. What Jesus is contradicting is not the law itself, but certain perversions of the law of which the scribes and Pharisees were guilty. Far from contradicting the law, Jesus endorses it, insists on its authority and supplies its true interpretation" (76). "It is these distortions of the law which Jesus rejected, not the law itself" (77). Stott provides four convincing arguments to prove this (76–78).

5. For a discussion on this topic, see G. K. Beale, ed., *The Right Doctrine From the Wrong Texts? Essays on the Use of the Old Testament in the New* (Grand Rapids, MI: Baker, 1994).

6. See Jiří Moskala, "The Decalogue in Luther and Adventism," in *Here We Stand: Luther, the Reformation, and Seventh-day Adventism*, ed. Michael W. Campbell and Nikolaus Satelmajer (Nampa, ID: Pacific Press®, 2017), 109–111.

7. Ellen G. White, *Christ's Object Lessons* (Battle Creek, MI: Review and Herald®, 1900), 333.

CHAPTER

Eight

Choose Life

The book of Deuteronomy contains Moses' three passionate farewell speeches before his death (Deuteronomy 1–4; 5–28; 29, 30). His last discourse springs from a loving heart and a deep devotion to the Lord. As a master preacher, Moses wishes the best for Israel in this sermon and fervently calls for the people's wholehearted service to the Lord. The Lord and Israel are pledged to exclusive loyalty and fidelity to each other, and Moses explains how such covenant faithfulness should be lived out by the believers. This sermon elaborates on the covenant and expounds on the loving covenantal relationship between God and His people.

God calls people to collaborate with Him, and His ultimate purpose in calling people to Himself is to save them (Exodus 19:4; Isaiah 45:22; Matthew 11:28, 29; John 12:32). Pharaoh and Cyrus are two classic illustrations of how God uses even mighty kings to accomplish His purposes. Cyrus, a positive example, collaborates with Him and becomes very successful (Isaiah 45:1–5), but Pharaoh is a negative model. The king of Egypt repeatedly despises God's Word to him and experiences only tragedies because he stubbornly opposes God's will (Exodus 5:1, 2; 12:29; 14:28; 15:3–5).

The third sermon: Sealing of the covenant at Moab

The third and last sermon is the shortest at only two chapters long (Deuteronomy 29; 30). But it is Moses' final heartfelt appeal for Israel to firmly decide to love God and obey His Torah. God is good to the Israelites, and this is the only way their future can be secured and their abundant life maintained. The Lord has made a covenant with them, and faithfulness to God will bring prosperity. Moses recapitulates and explains this covenant relationship and makes a special and lasting appeal.

Because Moses passionately calls for the Israelites to choose life, the book of Deuteronomy could be titled in the following way: "Choose life—Love, obey, and fear the Lord." The phrase "choose life" is taken from the conclusion of the last sermon (Deuteronomy 30:19).

This speech calls for action because Moses knows that he will be with them for only a short time. He is now 120 years old, and the last weeks of his earthly life are ahead of him. He knows this because the Lord has revealed it to him (Deuteronomy 4:21, 22; 31:2).

The key word in this discourse is "today" (Hebrew *hayyom*; literally, "the day"), which occurs fourteen times. (This word appears seventy-four times in the whole book.) Today is "the day" to decide. It evokes a sense of urgency. The Israelites should not delay their decision to sincerely follow and serve God. They need to do it now—today. Another key expression is "covenant," appearing in this section of the book seven times. These dynamics are all related to the God of the covenant who swore to give the land to Abraham, Isaac, and Jacob (Deuteronomy 30:20).

Moses' last speech may be divided into five sections:

1. Israel exhorted to accept the covenant (Deuteronomy 29:1–15).
   a. Retrospective summary: deliverance from Egypt, Exodus experience (Deuteronomy 29:1–8). Moses begins with the recapitulation of Israel's recent history and of God's mighty acts for His people. They have seen with their own eyes what

the Lord did for them in Egypt and how He miraculously brought them out of the land of slavery. Moses reminds them of what their loving Lord has done for them, not only giving them freedom but also graciously caring for them during their years in the wilderness where they have lacked nothing. God is their Creator and the Sustainer of life. In addition, He has proved to them His leadership by defeating two powerful kings in the Transjordan region—Sihon, the king of Heshbon, and Og, the king of Bashan. Moses has also underlined the defeat of these two kings in his first sermon (Deuteronomy 2:24–3:8).

b. Present generation: Appeal to renew the covenant (Deuteronomy 29:9–15). Everyone in the present generation needs to renew and confirm their commitment to God and "carefully follow the terms of this covenant" (verse 9, NIV) so the Lord will be their God (verse 13). Also, the future generations need to continue in their total dedication to Him (verses 14, 15).

2. Warning against future perils—disobedience will be punished (Deuteronomy 29:16–28).

a. Warning against idolatry (Deuteronomy 29:16–21). Moses continues his sermon with a strong caution against idolatry, defined as "bitter poison" (verse 18, NIV). Idolatry will be the Israelites' constant temptation. They need to be vigilant; otherwise, it will destroy their relationship with their Maker, uproot their prosperity, and lead them into detestable practices connected with false worship. Only curses will follow as a result.

b. A lesson for future generations (Deuteronomy 29:22–28). Israel's posterity needs to follow God's teaching in order to experience God's presence and blessing. If they abandon God's covenant, then disasters and calamities will accompany them, and the fate of Sodom and Gomorrah will await them. If they follow a wicked course of life, they will bring shame on their God. Other nations will overpower them, and they will be scattered among the nations and lose their homeland (Deuteronomy 30:1, 3, 5).

3. God's secrets and revealed things (Deuteronomy 29:29). At the center of the chiastically arranged discourse, Moses stresses the contrast between God and humans. God is omniscient; He knows hidden and secret things because He is the God of wisdom (Daniel 2:20–23, 28, 29, 47). Humans can only understand what God reveals to them, and what He discloses of His ways and will is sufficient for them to make the right decisions and obey and worship Him.
4. Apostasy and forgiveness (Deuteronomy 30:1–10). The God of Israel is a gracious and merciful God. If His people who are unfaithful will repent (Hebrew *shub*, "return, repent") and obey Him with all of their hearts, then the Lord will have compassion on them, restore their fortunes, and gather them back from all the nations (verses 2, 3). What a beautiful God of the Old Testament! He delights in His people and wants to prosper their work.
5. Final appeal to choose life and blessings (Deuteronomy 30:11–20). God's commands are easy to follow (verses 11–14) because He always enables people to obey them. They can follow their God because He is with them and has demonstrated that He loves them. This provides the right motivation and power to be connected to Him. Moses' culminating call for commitment is made through contrasts (verses 15–20). On the one side are death, destruction, and curses, while on the other side are life, prosperity, and blessings. This life-death antithesis is directly linked to the covenant blessings of life and curses (death). Spiritual warfare is in the background, so Moses pleads with the Israelites to choose life and a bright future with the Lord their God. He is very personal: God loves you, so now choose life so that you may live. What does choosing life mean? It means to

love the Lord (Hebrew *'ahab*; the plea to love Him is mentioned three times [verses 6, 16, 20]), listen (Hebrew *shama'*, "listen, obey") to His voice, and cling to Him (Hebrew *dabaq*, "hold fast, cling, attach, unite" [Genesis 2:24]). In a few words, Moses concludes his appeal: "I call heaven and earth to witness against you today, that I have set before you life and death, blessing and curse. Therefore choose life, that you and your offspring may live, loving the LORD your God, obeying his voice and holding fast to him, for he is your life and length of days, that you may dwell in the land that the LORD swore to your fathers, to Abraham, to Isaac, and to Jacob, to give them" (Deuteronomy 30:19, 20, ESV).

The pitfall of idolatry

God spoke to Israel from Horeb (Sinai), and everyone saw the solemn and magnificent display of His glory. But the Israelites did not see God's form; they only heard His voice (Deuteronomy 4:12, 13; 5:22). God chose this method of communication because He did not want them to create an idol of Him in any shape or form (Deuteronomy 4:15–24). God warned His people against idolatry, which is one of the roots of all evil and a grievous sin from which many vile things spring. Idolatry lies at the core of all the misery of God's people. Moses and the prophets used the strongest language to persuade people of its emptiness and addiction, but the people would not listen (Deuteronomy 4:16–19, 23; Isaiah 44:6–24; Jeremiah 4:1; 7:30; Ezekiel 5:11; 8:6; 20:7, 8, 18, 31).

It is shocking that idolatry was the greatest offense against God, yet God's people repeatedly fell into it.

"They sacrificed to demons, not to God,
To gods they did not know,
To new gods, new arrivals
That your fathers did not fear" (Deuteronomy 32:17, NKJV).

We often wonder why ancient believers were so naive and uncorrectable when they engaged in worshiping different man-made idols. We are quite sure that we would never do something like that. Really? Maybe not in the simplistic way of bowing down before objects, but what about being dependent on things or concepts that captivate our thinking and behavior?

Is it possible that idolatry is a danger for Adventists in today's postmodern world? A growing boy once said to his dad, "Daddy, I know which of God's commandments we never transgressed." His father was curious, and then he heard the explanation: "We never made or worshiped an idol; we have always obeyed God's command: 'You shall have no other gods before Me!' " With our first quick thought, we conclude that idolatry does not concern us. We might think that it is relevant only to Hindu people, but maybe we should think again. Is it so simple? The idols of today may have different shapes and forms yet a similar appeal. We do not easily admit that we could be slaves to the idols in our lives. We deny even the possibility that it might be a problem! While we might not have literal idols, we are easily drawn to popular TV shows, such as *American Idol.* So the question is worth asking: Are we really free of idols?

The key question, it seems, is, What is idolatry? And maybe more important is the question, What is so attractive about idolatry that we fall for it despite all of the warnings?

Idolatry is extremely dangerous and degrades God in people's eyes as well as it debases humanity. What you behold, you become (Psalm 115:8; Jeremiah 2:5; compare 2 Kings 17:15). Nothing in this life distracts and diverts our focus more than idols. Idolatry corrupts more than anything else. The Living God is put aside and replaced by the gods of human imagination. Idolatry destroys the true meaning of life in all directions. It degrades humans because what we worship has the biggest impact on our lives. The Creator God becomes a "puppy" in human hands, so we can manipulate Him. The pertinent question is, What preoccupies our thinking? In what patterns do we think? Do we follow Creation, Redemption, and re-creation reasoning or evolutionary thinking?

John strongly warns Christians: "Dear children, keep yourselves from idols" (1 John 5:21, NIV). This verse from John's epistle is surprising. Why does John need to admonish Christ's followers to say no to false gods and stay away from idols? In the Roman Empire, there were many cults with a multitude of literal idols, and even the Caesars proclaimed themselves to be gods. The fundamental question was, Whom should they follow—Christ or Caesar?

But in the modern setting, what do we mean by *idols*? An *idol* is something that replaces God, and even though we know it is not right, we still do it, often repeatedly. An *idol* is anything or anyone that captures our imagination, affection, time, and mind more than God. Idolatry is the opposite of a theocentric life. If God is not at the center of our lives, other gods will fill His place. If we do not enjoy and cultivate God's living presence in our lives, we will enjoy and devote our lives to something or somebody else. The substitution of Christ may have different appearances: pride, self-centeredness, money, power, sex, food, pleasures, work, sports, family, games, films, shopping, ideas, politics, position, degree, grades, and so forth. An *idol* is something that absorbs our affections and enslaves our thinking. It is always shallow. An idol steals our time, absorbs our concentration, and distracts us from true focus in life. So we serve it and follow its ideology, charm, and drive. You may be an idol worshiper if you check your emails or favorite websites before spending time with Jesus in the morning.

The problem is that humans are idol-making factories. We are creative and inventive in this regard. Drugs, alcohol, impure thoughts, cheating, pornography, video games, and music can be on the list of idols, which has no end! We are capable of turning everything good, beautiful, and meaningful into idols. Idolatry changes our personalities, the way of our thinking, our affections, and our social lives. It reshapes our identities and replaces genuine personal relationships with fake interactions.

So the question comes again, Who or what fills and controls our thinking? Remember that the great controversy starts in your brain. Ask yourself, Whom do I serve? You know that you cannot follow two masters! "Blessed is the one . . . whose delight is in the law of the LORD, and who meditates on his law day and night" (Psalm 1:1, 2, NIV).

During the day, you can test yourself with a pertinent question: What do I spend more time on—my God or something else? The diversions can be "innocent" or sinful and addictive. But whatever steals your time, affection, imagination, and desire away from enjoying God's presence in your thoughts becomes an idol, and you are on dangerous ground. Whatever captures your imagination more than God is your idol. Be brutally honest with yourself. Are you in tune with Him, or is something else replacing Him? If something is displacing God's primacy in your life, then you are on an extremely slippery slope.

Only a meaningful relationship with Christ can liberate us from our idolatrous addictions: "Then you will know the truth, and the truth will set you free" (John 8:32, NIV). Jesus invites us to Himself so He can change us: "Come to me, all you who are weary and burdened, and I will give you rest" (Matthew 11:28, NIV).

CHAPTER
Nine

Turn Their Hearts

In his farewell sermon, Moses makes a robust appeal to the people to choose life, stay on the right path, and be faithful to God and His covenant. Afterward, he passes the leadership torch to Joshua. According to God's instructions, Moses commissions Joshua to be the new leader of Israel (Deuteronomy 31:1–8, 14). Then before his death, Moses teaches the Israelites a song (Deuteronomy 32) and blesses the twelve tribes of Israel (Deuteronomy 33). It is interesting that only these two chapters, which are written in poetry, use different types of Hebrew parallelism (synonymous, antithetical, synthetic, emblematic, and comparative) with two or three parallel thoughts combined together (bicolons and tricolons). These are magnificent didactic poems, full of deep wisdom and insight, that also carry prophetic connotations.

Throughout the book, Moses uses vivid language, combining stories with legal material and song with history. Thus, the book of Deuteronomy contains multiple genres. Rhetorical expressions of the three sermons are mixed with covenantal language and tied with poetry. The legislative material is placed closely with narratives and exhortations. Blessings are presented together with many curses.[1] Punishments are associated with the law. This is understandable because the law is as strong as the consequences of trespassing it. This blend of blessings and curses sheds light on God's different actions and demonstrates that the God of Israel is a loving, merciful, and just God. He is the God of the covenant, the God of history, and the God of time and space.

This portrayal of God is particularly true in these two poems because the theology of Deuteronomy 32 and 33 elaborates on God's character, His teachings, and His law. This extraordinary design points to the literary genius behind this inspired magnum opus and demonstrates that Deuteronomy is a work of sacred art—a true masterpiece that reflects an intimate knowledge of God. Its theocentric thinking is consistent and reveals a pattern of longing for the prosperity and happiness of God's people. The thinking in it is thoroughly relational and anchored in God's love toward people. When Israel's affectionate leader concludes his works by breaking into poetry, he not only contributes to the beauty of God but also helps people to remember his words better.

The Song of Moses

Moses composed—or it is better to say, received from God—a song to teach Israel (Deuteronomy 31:19, 22). This song contains an outstanding, warm, and brilliant picture of God. In this song, Moses pleads with the Israelites to be faithful to their attractive God. It is his last attempt to turn their hearts to God, and it is extremely urgent because the Lord has just told him about Israel's future apostasy (Deuteronomy 31:16–21; compare verses 27–29). Moses' heart must be breaking, yet he tries everything within his power to reverse this tendency of forgetting the Lord and seeks to help God's people hold fast to their God and not depart from Him. Their hearts need to be circumcised (Deuteronomy 10:16, NIV), not just their flesh, in order for them to adhere to the Lord, listen to His voice, and keep His commandments. It means that they need to love and live with the

Lord, experience His goodness, and respond to Him with wholehearted service. Moses puts his appeal into a song, which is one of the best emotional devices to remember thoughts and embrace them.

In the Song of Moses, God's names and epithets are multifaceted and form an insightful mosaic of who He is. God is painted as the Lord (Deuteronomy 32:3, 12, 30), the Rock (verses 4, 15, 18, 30, 31), the Father (verse 6), the Creator (verse 6), the Most High (verse 8), the Eagle (verse 11), the Savior (verse 15), and the Life (verse 47). In his blessings, Moses adds that God is also Israel's King (Deuteronomy 33:5), Refuge (verse 27), Shield (verse 29, NIV), Helper (verse 29, NIV), and glorious Sword (verse 29, NIV). This medley of titles speaks volumes about God's beautiful character. All of His designations are positive. Indeed, there are no rival gods because idols are man-made gods, which are projections of people's fears and imagination. The true God is the Creator of everything. He is the incomparable Living God. "There is no one like the God of Jeshurun[2]" (verse 26, NIV). It is easy to follow such a good God, who is always for His people. Moses' very last words to Israel before his death testify to this truth:

> "Blessed are you, Israel!
>   Who is like you,
>   a people saved by the LORD?
> He is your shield and helper
>   and your glorious sword.
> Your enemies will cower before you,
>   and you will tread on their heights" (verse 29, NIV).

Moses declares, "Praise the greatness of our God!" (Deuteronomy 32:3, NIV). He also states that God's "works are perfect, and all his ways are just" (verse 4, NIV), and He is "a faithful God who does no wrong, upright and just is he" (verse 4, NIV). The God of the Old Testament is the Creator, Sovereign Lord, Savior, King, Judge, Prophet, and Priest.

The verbs of His actions are powerful. The God of Israel is the One "who made you and formed you" (verse 6, NIV), "gave the nations their inheritance . . . set up boundaries for the peoples" (verse 8, NIV), "fathered you; . . . gave you birth" as your Mother (verse 18, NIV), puts to death and brings to life (verse 39, NIV), and makes "atonement for his land and people" (verse 43, NIV). The eternal God is also jealous and angered by idolatry. He scatters, wounds, blots out, repays, and hides His face when people stubbornly follow their wicked ways, unwilling to repent. He shields, cares, guards, creates, feeds, nourishes, judges, avenges, heals, brings to life, delivers, forgives, and atones. But above all, this gracious God loves His people (Deuteronomy 33:3), and that is why He disciplines them (Deuteronomy 4:36; compare Exodus 20:20).

All of these epithets and descriptions are significant because they point to different aspects of God's roles and functions. But no human language or categories can exhaustively describe God because He is larger than our vocabularies and classifications can grasp. God is all these and much more. He transcends all we can say about Him, for He is always more beautiful, gracious, greater, and nicer than we can imagine. During all of eternity, we will study the science of God's character, what He accomplished during His incarnation, His death on the cross, and beyond. We will continually marvel at His character of love, truth, holiness, justice, and beauty.

A shining example of this God in action is Deuteronomy 32's designation of Him as an Eagle. It is a powerful image of God being like a parent. He is a Parent who cares for His children as an eagle "hovers" over its eaglets to protect them and teach them to fly and hunt (verse 11). (The verb "hover" is also used in the biblical Creation story where "the Spirit of God was hovering over the surface of the waters" to sustain God's creation and take care of the newborn planet Earth [Genesis 1:2].) Similar eagle imagery is used by the Lord Himself in Exodus 19:4, where He explains to Israel what they have experienced: "You know how I carried you on eagles' wings and brought you to myself." Jesus may have had this eagle symbolism in mind when He said how much He wanted to gather Israel as a mother hen gathers her chicks (Matthew 23:37). But He changed the imagery from an eagle to a hen because the image of an eagle would have been misunderstood. The Romans used the symbol of the eagle to express their dominance, authority, and power. Jesus wisely changed the politically charged image of the eagle to that of a hen in order to convey His beautiful message of love, care, and protection. Tragically, Christ had to conclude that Israel was not willing to submit to His loving and merciful leadership.

The blessings of Moses

God is calling people to Himself because He wants to bless them. The priests were to pronounce blessings over Israel, but God Himself blessed them when the priests recited the benedictions over the people (Numbers 6:23–27). Thus, Moses invokes God's blessings upon the Israelite tribes. The poetic blessings of Deuteronomy 33 resemble Jacob's blessings before his death (Genesis 49). The sequence of tribal names in Deuteronomy differs from that of Jacob's list, which was enumerated according to their birth order. Moses' sequence is guided somewhat by geography (from Reuben in the Transjordan, extending to the western tribes, to end with the northern tribes of Naphtali and Asher in the Galilee region) and by their mothers (the first three tribes are from Leah's sons; the following two are Rachel's sons; then come Leah's last two sons; and, finally, the sons of Bilhah and Zilpah in mixed order). It is interesting that Joseph is blessed (the longest of the blessings) together with his two sons, Ephraim and Manasseh, but Simeon's tribe is omitted, probably because it was situated within Judah's territory.

Significantly, Moses begins his blessings by emphasizing God's self-revelation at Sinai (verse 2). The Israelites' well-being will depend upon their obedience to Him and His Word. The Lord loves His people (verse 3) and is their King (verse 5). The unity of all the tribes is thus stressed before Moses speaks about the individual tribes represented by Jacob's specific sons. The core of Moses' blessing is for Judah, Levi, and Joseph, where two prophecies regarding the Messiah are located.

Deuteronomy's last poem also captures the Messianic hope. In the immediate context of these blessings, it is explained that because of people's disobedience disaster will happen "in the latter days" (Deuteronomy 31:29, NKJV) or "in days to come" (NIV), alluding to the future and the end of days. Moses predicts that the *khasid* (the "faithful," "godly," "loyal," "pious," or "Holy One"), whom the Thummim and Urim rightly belong to, will come—the One who was "tested at Massah" and "contended at the waters of Meribah" (Deuteronomy 33:8, NIV). Verse 16 has a similar Messianic allusion that speaks of the *nazir* (the "separated," "consecrated," or "prince") as the one separated from, or the one consecrated among, his brothers. These texts point to the Messiah coming from priestly and royal lines. Thus, the Pentateuch ends with the perspective of the Messianic hope.

Power to obey comes only from God

Repeatedly, Moses admonishes Israel to obey the Lord their God. The good news is that whatever God commands, He enables His followers to do. The prophet Ezekiel explains this thought in the core of his theological summary in Ezekiel 36:26, 27: "I will give you a new heart and put a new spirit within you; I will take the heart of stone out of your flesh and give you a heart of flesh. I will put My Spirit within you and cause you to walk in My statutes, and you will keep My judgments and do them" (NKJV).

To change a human heart is solely the work of God. He can only transform our hearts by removing our hearts of stone and replacing them with sensitive hearts of flesh. As Joshua reminds his audience, we are not able to obey God: "You are not able to serve the LORD" (Joshua 24:19). We can only decide for Him and for what is right. This is our crucial role. But we do not have the power to accomplish our decision. In our fragility and weakness, we need help from outside of ourselves. But we are not left in despair; when we give our weaknesses to God, He provides the willingness (which is a response to His call of love) and power to obey (Philippians 2:13). He is able to make us strong, and the Holy Spirit will move us to obey Him. Paul says, "When I am weak, then I am strong" (2 Corinthians 12:10; compare 1 Corinthians 10:13; 1 Thessalonians 5:23, 24; 2 Thessalonians 3:3; Jude 24).

God gathers, cleanses, removes sin, gives, puts, and moves us to carefully keep His law (Ezekiel 36:24–30). What He is doing, we will do when we let Him be the Lord of our lives. He identifies with us, and if we associate closely with Him, His doing will be our active doing. The unity between God and us will be dynamic, powerful, and lively. Good work is accomplished only through the power of the Holy Spirit!

The emphasis in Ezekiel 36:27 is on God's doing. The literal translation reads, "I will give My Spirit in you, and I will do that you will walk in My statutes and keep My laws, and you will do." Thus, God promises, "I will do that you will do! I will move and cause you to obey!" In other words, God commands people to obey, and He will help them do so. He will give them His Spirit to accomplish His will because obedience is performed only through the power of the Holy Spirit. God makes obedience happen. What God commands, He provides! What God requires of His people, He always helps them do.

Obedience is God's gift—not our performance or achievement—just as justification and salvation are His gifts too. All is given by God's grace and is received through faith. When God's Word and His Spirit are accepted, genuine spiritual living occurs (Ezekiel 37:11–14). Then Christ and His grace can reign in our hearts, bringing peace and joy to all of our relationships. This is the gospel par excellence!

1. "Blessing formulae are normally used less than curses. For example, the Law Collection of Hammurabi (1792–1750 BC) only has two blessings, but has fifty curses. In the biblical material, Exodus/Leviticus has 10 curses to 5 blessings, Deuteronomy has forty curses to eight blessings." Paul Lawrence, *The Books of Moses Revisited* (Eugene, OR: Wipf & Stock, 2011), 76.

2. It is ironic that the specific term designating Israel in this poem is *Jeshurun*, meaning "upright one" (mentioned only four times in the Bible: Deuteronomy 32:15; 33:5, 26; Isaiah 44:2). In the song's context, the one who should walk straight with the Lord turns out to be full of unfaithfulness and apostasy.

CHAPTER

Ten

Remember, Do Not Forget

One of the most troubling and worst sins of God's people in biblical times was (and unfortunately still is) forgetfulness. In order to prevent forgetting, the book of Deuteronomy underlines the importance of remembering and testifies as to how the Lord led Israel in the past. But after a time, believers easily forget God's mighty deeds on their behalf, take them for granted and do not appreciate them. They become normal, assumed, and common, and they evaporate from memory. This is why Scripture admonishes us to actively remember God, His ways, and His leadership. God wants us to seek and value fresh insights through His goodness as demonstrated toward His people. His providence, grace, care, and faithfulness are proven by His past actions, and we should not forget them.

Among the key words used in Deuteronomy is the Hebrew term *shakakh*, meaning "forget." This crucial expression appears only fourteen times in this book (Deuteronomy 4:9, 23, 31; 6:12; 8:11, 14, 19 [twice]; 9:7; 25:19; 26:13; 31:21; 32:18 [the word is used once in the sense of forgetting or overlooking a sheaf: 24:19]). Israel's forgetfulness of God and of what is right is a dominant feature during the journey from Egypt—the land where they were enslaved. Moses stresses that the Lord their God is a merciful God, and He will not forget them and the covenant He has made with them (Deuteronomy 4:31). He strongly admonishes that the Israelites should then not forget their God: "Only be careful, and watch yourselves closely so that you do not forget the things your eyes have seen or let them fade from your heart as long as you live. Teach them to your children and to their children after them. Remember the day you stood before the LORD your God at Horeb, when he said to me, 'Assemble the people before me to hear my words so that they may learn to revere me as long as they live in the land and may teach them to their children' " (verses 9, 10, NIV). This ancient problem of forgetfulness is also a modern problem, unfortunately. It seems that we especially have a lack of memory in the spiritual realm.

Another key expression in the book of Deuteronomy is the Hebrew word *zakar*, signifying "remember," which occurs fifteen times (Deuteronomy 5:15; 7:18 [twice]; 8:2, 18; 9:7, 27; 15:15; 16:3, 12; 24:9, 18, 22; 25:17; 32:7). Remembrance is the opposite of amnesia, and it points to maintaining in our memory God's acts of kindness, love, and care; His goodness toward His people; and His leadership. Moses reminds Israel of what God has done in their favor in the past (Deuteronomy 1–4) and admonishes them to stay faithful to the Lord and keep the covenant in the new land they will inherit. He reiterates God's faithfulness and His love and that they should faithfully respond to Him by having Him as their only God and lovingly observing His laws. The corpus of God's law is then carefully explained in Deuteronomy 5–26. Moses follows this with a strong admonishment to faithfulness in the form of blessings and curses (Deuteronomy 27–30).

In order to remember God, Israel needed to hear the Word of God (Deuteronomy 4:1; 5:1; 6:4; 9:1) and follow it (Deuteronomy 4:2, 40; 5:10, 29; 6:27; 8:1; etc.). The Hebrew verb *shama'* has two complementary meanings: (1) "hear," "listen," and (2) "obey." A person who hears and understands God's teaching will follow His instruction—that is, he or she will obey. The term *shama'* occurs ninety-one times in the book of Deuteronomy, and out of these occurrences, it is used as a command "hear" six times (Deuteronomy 4:1; 5:1; 6:4; 9:1; 20:3; 33:7). The closely related word *shamar*, translated mainly as "keep," "observe," or "be careful," is employed seventy-three times (for example, Deuteronomy 4:2, 40; 5:10, 29; 6:25; 7:9; 8:11; 11:8, 22; 12:28; 27:1; 30:10, 16; 31:12; 32:46; 33:9). From these statistics, it is evident that Moses underscores obedience to God and His Word. When we personally know God and appreciate His acts of love on our behalf, we will then follow His instructions with joy out of gratitude for His goodness toward us.

Deuteronomy 8 and 9 deal especially with the issue of staying in a relationship with God by carefully remembering His actions: "Remember how the LORD your God led you all the way in the wilderness these forty years" (Deuteronomy 8:2, NIV). "Be careful that you do not forget the LORD your God, failing to observe his commands, his laws and his decrees that I am giving you this day" (verse 11, NIV). "But remember the LORD your God. He gives you the ability to produce wealth" (verse 18, NIrV). "Remember this and never forget how you aroused the anger of the LORD your God in the wilderness" (Deuteronomy 9:7, NIV). It is also interesting that Moses calls on God to remember His promises to the patriarchs because, in spite of the Israelites' fragility and rebellion, they are His people: "Remember your servants, Abraham, Isaac, and Jacob. Do not regard the stubbornness of this people, or their wickedness or their sin. . . . For they are your people and your heritage, whom you brought out by your great power and by your outstretched arm" (verses 27, 29, ESV).

The grievous sins that God's people had committed in the past demonstrated that they had very short memories and easily forgot what God did for them. It means they did not treasure His leadership and did not cherish His mighty acts on their behalf. The sin of God's people was forgetting the Lord, His covenant, His commandments, and His leading. James states, "If anyone, then, knows the good they ought to do and doesn't do it, it is sin" (James 4:17). This is why the

Bible emphasizes the importance of memory.

Perhaps you have heard about the World Memory Championships or the USA Memory Championship. Those who participate in these events have phenomenal memories. In a few minutes, they can memorize information the rest of us would have difficulty learning in a long period of time. For example, within five minutes, they are able to memorize a list of computer-generated numbers presented in a row of twenty digits with twenty-five rows per page. Competitors must start with the first digit in the first row and continue through the consecutive rows. Skipping rows is not permitted. What phenomenal memories! But we are dealing with much more than a memory competition—our eternal life depends on remembering God. In our hectic everyday lives, how do we remember what God is doing for us? Do we appreciate His guidance in our lives? Are we grateful for it?

Life without memory

Imagine life without memories or with a poor memory. What would that mean? *Memory* is usually defined as the "ability to remember events and experience."[1] The *New Encyclopaedia Britannica* describes *memory* as "the retention and retrieval in the human mind of past experience."[2] Let me describe several crucial consequences of losing one's memory, and in this way, I will demonstrate its importance.

First, without memories, there can be no history or understanding of the past. Things, facts, events, data, and experiences are forgotten and lost. Humanity would not know its origin, its glorious beginning, and the flow of history. Thus, the first basic philosophical question—Where do we come from?—would be a great puzzle for us, and no solution would be available. Without memory, there is not deep (and /or lasting) thinking and development of one's thoughts.

Memory disorders cause major complications. Millions of people are affected by the painful and deadly results of Alzheimer's disease—one of the most devastating forms of memory loss. It is an irreversible and progressive brain disorder that slowly destroys one's thinking skills. The first episode of the documentary series *The Alzheimer's Project* profiles seven people who are living with an advancing state of dementia caused by the disease—from its earliest detectable changes to death.[3] This sickness touches people deeply on physical, emotional, and mental levels, and it affects their spiritual integrity. One can physically function well without memory, but this kind of life could be described as mental nonexistence. The spiritual loss of memory is even more serious because it means not knowing the Lord and valuing what He is doing.

Second, without memories, there can be no lessons learned from history. History helps us to learn from the struggles, defeats, and victories of God's people in the past; if history did not exist for us, we would be doomed to repeat those mistakes. This is why Jews commemorate the victims and survivors of the Holocaust and maintain Holocaust museums in order not to forget past atrocities made on ethnic grounds and to avoid their repetition.

Memory plays a crucial role in different key functions of life: "Learning, thought, and reasoning could not occur without remembering."[4] Without memory, we would be constant learners without the ability to learn anything. Thus, we would be destined for failure.

Have you ever thought of what would happen if the Bible were wiped out of physical existence and from people's memories? Fortunately, Holy Scripture presents God's "memory": Scripture is a record of His will and the plan of salvation in the context of the great controversy. It secures the memory of God's people, their history, their struggles, and the final triumph He will give them.

Third, without memories, there can be no understanding of the present. Lacking memories, we would not know the answer to the second philosophical question—Why are we here? Without memories, our whole existence would be in danger because we would live only for a given moment and for pleasure, entertainment, food, and power. Life's motto would then reflect only the experiential dimension—carpe diem! Without memories, only the present reality remains, but the present immediately evaporates; it almost does not exist because "now" changes instantly into the past.

Fourth, without memories, there can be no future. Understanding the future would be impossible, and any perspective on future events would be lost. This also means that the third basic philosophical question would have no answer: we would not know where we go. Prophecies would have no meaning because God's prophecies have been established by His mighty acts in the past. Remembering the future hope is possible only if there is a remembrance of God's fulfilled promises and predictions from the past.

Fifth, without memories, there can be no hope, like darkness in a tunnel without a beam of light ahead of us. Jeremiah aptly declares, "I call to mind [the Lord's love and compassion] and therefore I have hope" (Lamentations 3:21, NIV). Hope only comes as a result of remembering God's gracious past activities for His people and humanity.

Sixth, without memories, there can be no gratitude, and without thankfulness, life is bereft of color. Only when we recall the love, goodness, kindness, patience, forgiveness, restoration, healings, and faithfulness of God can we cultivate a sense of appreciation and build a meaningful relationship with Him. Only when the kind deeds of our Lord are fresh in our minds can they generate the right motives.

Seventh, without memories, there can be no obedience because we need to discern God's will by meditating on His law of love in order to faithfully follow Him.

Eighth, without memories, we cannot retain our identities. I am sure you have heard about people who have lost their memories. By losing their memories, they no longer know who they are and to whom they belong. Our memories retain past and present dimensions of time and the richness of time.

Isaiah solemnly declares, "The former things will not be remembered, nor will they come to mind" (Isaiah 65:17b, NIV; see also

Revelation 21:1, 4b). What does this mean? It cannot refer to the loss of memory because people with amnesia lose their own identities and become changed people with different behaviors. In addition, if the redeemed do not remember the lessons learned from the great controversy, sin could enter the world once again, and the whole conflict between good and evil would have been in vain.

But God wants to heal our memories! Our former painful lives will be no more. Our memories will be at peace; our pasts will be healed. We will not be haunted, troubled, or bothered by our past sins, hurts, mistakes, abuse, unfinished duties, and problems because we will have gone through the process of reconciliation. Harmony, peace, and joy will be restored. We will no longer be slaves of our past transgressions and deep emotional wounds. No painful flashbacks will irritate us. Thus, our healthy memories will be restored, and our painful pasts will no more be burdens. Such healed minds will be filled with peace and joy.

Ninth, without memories, there can be no meaningful relationships. With no memories, love cannot exist. Dementia destroys fellowship. People who have lost their memories do not recognize their loved ones, their spouses, or their own children. The second episode of *The Alzheimer's Project*, titled "Grandpa, Do You Know Who I Am?" is geared toward children and young teens coping with a grandparent with Alzheimer's disease and the grandparent's gradual memory decline.[5] Ultimately, the episode shows how important it is to handle a grandparent's loss of memory with kindness, patience, and compassion.

Tenth, without memories, there can be no faith. Atheism or empty routine religious practices are a logical result of memory loss. Nothing supernatural is recognized by people who live in the moment and by their natural instincts.

Remember—do not forget

Memory is a heavenly gift, and our identities and orientation in life, as well as our moral, spiritual, emotional, and social lives, depend on its proper function. Ellen White rightly explains: "These are the things we are never to forget. The love of Jesus, with its constraining power, is to be kept fresh in our memory. . . . His sacrifice is the center of our hope. Upon this we must fix our faith."[6]

If we had no memories, everything we are doing and planning to do would be futile and in vain. Therefore, it is vital to keep the history of God's activities and His people alive for the healthy identity and future of the church.

We need to exercise our memories in order to have sufficient memory banks in our minds. One way to keep our memories alert is by memorizing Scripture. Meditate on God's powerful promises and study His mighty acts in history (Joshua 1:6–9; Psalm 1:1–3). This will help you remember God's goodness and cultivate His presence in your life. No wonder Moses placed such a heavy emphasis upon remembering. Praise the Lord for the gift of memory! Let us exercise it well.

---

1. *Longman Dictionary of American English* (1983), s.v. "memory."
2. *The New Encyclopaedia Britannica*, 15th ed. (2010), s.v. "memory."
3. *The Alzheimer's Project*, episode 1, "The Memory Loss Tapes," directed by Shari Cookson and Nick Doob, aired May 10, 2009, on HBO.
4. *New Encyclopaedia Britannica*, s.v. "memory."
5. *The Alzheimer's Project*, episode 2, "Grandpa, Do You Know Who I Am?" directed by Eamon Harrington and John Watkin, written by Maria Shriver, aired May 11, 2009, on HBO.
6. Ellen G. White, *The Desire of Ages* (Mountain View, CA: Pacific Press®, 1982), 660.

CHAPTER

Eleven

Deuteronomy in the Later Writings

Moses is distinguished in the Scriptures as the servant of the Lord (Deuteronomy 34:5; Joshua 1:1, 2, 7, 15; Nehemiah 9:14). God calls him "my servant" (Joshua 1:2), which means that Moses was always ready to fulfill God's will. He was in the service of his King, Master, and Lord.

Moses as a model prophet

Moses is also described as God's friend with whom the Lord communicated face to face (Exodus 33:11; Deuteronomy 34:10). He communicated the will of God to Israel (Acts 7:38) and interceded for sinners (Exodus 32:30, 31). Thus, he was a model prophet (Deuteronomy 18:15, 18; 34:10), a symbol of religious authority in Israel, and a standard for all other prophets. Anyone with a message from God was measured against Moses and his instructions. In order to be accepted, the teachings of other prophets needed to be in harmony with God's words as revealed to and recorded by Moses.

Moses, who murdered an Egyptian guard and was despised by his own people at first (Exodus 2:11, 12, 14), chose to stay and suffer with God's people (Hebrews 11:25, 27), eventually becoming a great leader.

Shortly after the Exodus, instead of talking to the rock at Kadesh, he struck the rock twice (Numbers 20:11, 12; Deuteronomy 32:51). This action robbed God of His glory, and Moses was not allowed to enter the Promised Land. But after his death, God's Word characterizes Moses as a person who was very close to God, highly esteemed, and a prototype for others to emulate: "Since then, no prophet has risen in Israel like Moses, whom the Lord knew face to face" (Deuteronomy 34:10, NIV).

Crucial role of the Torah

Moses' writings had a deep impact and lasting influence on later holy texts. The Pentateuch was considered the highest authority, and everything else was evaluated against Moses' teachings. The Torah was the Magna Carta for teaching and ethics and for faith and practice (Psalm 1; Proverbs 3); thus, it was praised by psalmists (Psalms 19; 119) and uplifted by the prophet Isaiah (Isaiah 1:10; 5:24; 8:19, 20; 30:9; 51:7).

The Torah is an anthology of God's instructions and His teachings. The Hebrew word *torah* is derived from the root *yarah*, which means to point with a finger to the right path or the direction in which people should walk. (It is significant that the Hebrew term for *sin* is *khatah*, which means to go astray from the path, walk away from God's directions, or miss the target. The Greek word *hamartia* carries the same meaning for sin.) Another word that is closely related to *torah* is the Hebrew verb *horah*, "to teach," "to instruct." When someone follows God's Word, His advice, and His teaching, that person walks in obedience because he walks on God's recommended path. This philosophy of life was presented by Moses, and later, it was embraced by other biblical authors, who encouraged people to obey and walk in God's way.

Numbers 12:6–8 plainly explains the authority of a prophet in comparison with the ministry of Moses. God Himself stated,

"When there is a prophet among you,

I, the Lord, reveal myself to them in visions,
I speak to them in dreams.
But this is not true of my servant Moses;
he is faithful in all my house.
With him I speak face to face,
clearly and not in riddles;
he sees the form of the Lord.
Why then were you not afraid
to speak against my servant Moses?" (NIV).

Moses was a prophet par excellence and became a norm for all later prophets. "All prophetic utterances were to be tested by God's revelation to Moses."[1] He was uplifted to this level as a prophet because (1) God communicated with him very closely, as with a friend, to reveal His Torah (Exodus 33:11; Deuteronomy 34:10); (2) he was God's faithful servant and is called "the servant of the Lord" (Deuteronomy 34:5; Joshua 1:1, 2, NKJV; compare Exodus 14:31; Numbers 12:7, 8; Hebrews 3:2, 5); (3) he performed mighty deeds, "miraculous signs and wonders" through the power of God (Deuteronomy 34:11, 12); (4) he was a mediator of the covenant at Sinai (Exodus 19:3–8; 20:18–20; 24:3–8); (5) he organized the Old Testament church more fully: after the Exodus, Israel became one nation; (6) he had several important roles assigned by God—leadership, speaking, and writing; and (7) he remained humble in spite of his high position. Even though his superior talent surpassed others', "Moses was a very humble man, more humble than anyone else on the face of the earth" (Numbers 12:3, NIV). Thus, his ministry was normative, and other prophets were compared to him and his teachings.

Moses brought God's presence with him wherever he went. Abraham Heschel states, "The prophet claims to be far more than a messenger. He is a person who stands in the presence of God (Jer. 15:19), who stands 'in the council of the Lord' (Jer. 23:18), who is a participant, as it were, in the council of God, not a bearer of dispatches whose function is limited to being sent on errands. He is a counselor as well as messenger."[2] Through the prophets, the invisible God becomes audible. Prophets make God's presence more real; they declare that they were in His presence. Samuel Meier states that "only the prophet ever made the claim that he stood in the presence of God."[3] Abraham Heschel observes that a prophet's task was to bring people into the presence of God. "They could not use the language of *essence*; they had to use the language of *presence*. They did not try to depict Him; they tried to present Him, to make Him present. In such an effort only words of grandeur and intensity, not abstractions, can be of any avail."[4]

Reflections in the Old Testament

Moses' overall writings are special, but Deuteronomy is the climax of the Pentateuch, setting the tone for the rest of the Hebrew Bible. Here are a few examples of how the book of Deuteronomy is reflected in other parts of the Old Testament.

Scholars recognize that the theology of the book of Deuteronomy had a tremendous influence on the historical books (Joshua, Judges, 1 and 2 Samuel, and 1 and 2 Kings), prophetic books (for example, Hosea, Jeremiah, and Ezekiel), and wisdom literature, of either polemical (Job or Ecclesiastes) or affirmative types (Proverbs). The law of life, of sowing and reaping, is presented in Deuteronomy in a clear-cut way: if a person loves and obeys the Lord, blessing follows; if one disobeys God's instructions, curses happen. (A more complex understanding of blessings and curses in life is presented in Job, Psalm 73, and Habakkuk.)

The Lord commanded Joshua: "Be strong and very courageous. Be careful to obey all the law my servant Moses gave you; do not turn from it to the right or to the left, that you may be successful wherever you go. Keep this Book of the Law always on your lips; meditate on it day and night, so that you may be careful to do everything written in it. Then you will be prosperous and successful" (Joshua 1:7, 8, NIV).

The "Book of the Law" (*torah*) is the book of Deuteronomy, but it goes beyond Deuteronomy to include everything Moses wrote—namely, the Pentateuch in its first, original form. (Moses is mentioned as a writer in Exodus 24:4; 34:27, 28; Numbers 33:2; 31:9, 24, 25.) The admonition to be strong and courageous also appears in Deuteronomy (Deuteronomy 31:6, 7, 23; compare Joshua 10:25). David repeats the same words to Solomon (1 Chronicles 28:20), and King Hezekiah does likewise with the Israelites before the battle with the Assyrians (2 Chronicles 32:7). The warning not to turn "to the right or to the left" from God's law is also mentioned in Deuteronomy (Deuteronomy 5:32; 17:11, 20; 28:14; compare Deuteronomy 2:27).

Later authors used Moses' phrase "walk in obedience," meaning literally "to walk in His [God's] ways" (Deuteronomy 5:33; 8:6; 10:12; 11:22; 19:9; 26:17; 28:9; 30:16, NIV). One can find similar phrases in Joshua 22:5; 1 Kings 2:3; 3:14; 8:58; 11:33, 38; 2 Kings 21:22; 2 Chronicles 6:31; 31:21; Psalm 128:1; Jeremiah 7:23; and Zechariah 3:7, NIV. The Lord requires that His followers, out of love for Him, pay attention to His instruction and walk in the path He has appointed. In doing this, they will be led to prosperity and success.

Samuel accepted the Exodus story as a historical and factual event (1 Samuel 12:6–8). When Solomon was inaugurated as king over Israel, David charged him with observing "what the Lord your God requires: Walk in obedience to him, and keep his decrees and commands, his laws and regulations, as written in the Law of Moses" (1 Kings 2:3, NIV).

In 622 BC, a fresh reading of the book of Deuteronomy sparked a reformation in Judaea during the reign of Josiah, who was its last godly king. This young ruler implemented this teaching in practical life and got rid of the idols in Judah, even though he had already begun a reformation earlier (2 Chronicles 34:3–13). Two biblical passages—2 Kings 22:3–23:25 and 2 Chronicles 34:14–33—describe how the priests discovered the forgotten book, the "Book of the Covenant" (2 Kings 23:2, NIV) in Jerusalem's temple. Its reading brought further revival and reformation. It is amazing how a godly leader, in close collaboration with priests and other leaders, can influence many for good and help them follow God's right path.

In Ezekiel 16, a beautiful woman represents Israel, which also resembles the story line of Deuteronomy 32, where God took loving care of His people (identified as Jacob in verse 9), tenderly providing everything for them (verses 10–15a). As often happened, the people turned from God to idols and foreign gods (verses 5, 15b–18), yet the Lord continued to work with them. Sadly, in the end, He was forced to reject them because they stubbornly rejected Him. Despite their unfaithfulness, God, in His mercy, showed grace and ultimately made "atonement" for His people (verse 43, NIV).

Ezekiel 16's parable of the foundling girl is a moving narrative—something like the story of a prodigal daughter. She is adopted into a family, and her new loving father takes care of everything in her life. He marries her as a grown-up, when she is a beautiful and attractive lady. He surrounds her with exceeding riches and fine fabrics, and she becomes a queen. But she does not appreciate his love and care, and her ingratitude leads to a lustful, wild, and promiscuous lifestyle that results in great disgrace and infuriates her husband. She is told that her lovers will turn against her and severely punish her. Instead of being punished by her husband, she receives blazing grace and unselfish love. The shocking, forgiving behavior of her husband culminates with the establishment of a new and eternal covenant that should overwhelm her and bring her back to her senses.

In this parable, the Lord Himself is the Father of this prodigal daughter and the Husband of the unfaithful wife. Israel should repent and live a radically different life because God wants to be the nation's Lord. At the end of this complicated love story, God, in His mercy, makes atonement (verse 63), culminating with His special care for His unfaithful wife. (Here, as in Deuteronomy 32:43, the crucial Hebrew word *kapar* is used.) Atonement brings expiation, purification, forgiveness, reconciliation, and restoration. God Himself is the Priest and

Expiación

makes atonement for His disloyal and unfaithful people.

A prophet speaks for God

The authority of a prophet is derived from God, His revelation, and His Word. The prophetic office is not bought or inherited but given from above. If a prophet is called by God, he or she has authority like Moses and speaks the very word of God that needs to be obeyed. When a prophet speaks, it is like God speaking because he or she delivers God's Word and not his or her own (2 Peter 1:19–21). Deuteronomy 18:17–19 describes why a prophet has authority and must be highly respected: "The Lord said to me: 'What they say is good. I will raise up for them a prophet like you from among their fellow Israelites, and I will put my words in his mouth. He will tell them everything I command him. I myself will call to account anyone who does not listen to my words that the prophet speaks in my name' " (NIV).

The proclamation of God's Word is crucial because the orthodoxy and genuineness of a subsequent prophet can be confirmed by examining his or her words (Isaiah 8:19, 20). The prophet's words establish the spiritual and visionary role of that prophet. Anyone can claim to have a special revelation from God, but the prophet's words are tangible and can be evaluated and judged. They can be measured against the previous revelation to see whether there are any contradictions.

Deuteronomy 13:1–4 describes the necessary truthfulness and credibility of a prophet's message. This passage states that even false prophets can perform miracles, and prophets working wonders can mislead. Mighty deeds and miracles are not proof of the trustworthiness and authenticity of the prophecy or the prophet's teachings. "One impossibility for a true biblical prophet, therefore, is that he would proclaim any message that promotes other gods and their worship."[5] "The signs or wonders the prophet performs are of secondary importance to the message they accompany."[6] "A person is not necessarily a prophet because he is able to announce a sign or wonder that comes to pass.

If the message that person speaks calls people to faithful obedience to the God of the Scriptures, only then should the sign or wonder be acknowledged as legitimate."[7]

The principle is thus clear: the prophetic message must be in harmony with God's previous revelation, and the new message cannot contradict the basic principles of what the Torah of Moses and other prophets have taught. The gift of the Spirit as demonstrated by the fruit of the Spirit is the genuine sign of truth: "Not everyone who says to me, 'Lord, Lord,' will enter the kingdom of heaven, but only the one who does the will of my Father who is in heaven. Many will say to me on that day, 'Lord, Lord, did we not prophesy in your name, and in your name drive out demons and in your name perform many miracles?' Then I will tell them plainly, 'I never knew you. Away from me, you evildoers!' " (Matthew 7:21–23, NIV).

The type of Christ

Since the time of Moses, every prophet has been compared to him to see whether his or her life and teachings are in harmony with the standard Moses set. But Jesus Christ, the Prophet with a capital *P*, is the only Prophet who surpassed Moses and is without comparison or parallel. Moses was a type of the Lord Jesus Christ because he faithfully communicated God's Word, interceded for sinners, and led God's people through many difficulties to the Promised Land. But people were not to look to him but look forward to a Prophet like Moses and obey Him. Deuteronomy 18:15 points to this Messianic hope: "The Lord your God will raise up for you a prophet like me from among you, from your fellow Israelites. You must listen to him."

At Pentecost, Peter highlighted this point in his sermon (Acts 3:17–23). The fulfillment of this prediction was realized in Christ. He is our hope—and the true Spokesperson for God, the true Prophet, and the wise Teacher in Israel. This is why we daily commit our lives to Him and choose to become His disciples.

1. Willem A. VanGemeren, *Interpreting the Prophetic Word: An Introduction to the Prophetic Literature of the Old Testament* (Grand Rapids, MI: Zondervan, 1990), 38.

2. Abraham J. Heschel, *The Prophets*, vol. 1 (New York: Harper & Row, 1962), 21.

3. Samuel A. Meier, *Themes and Transformations in Old Testament Prophecy* (Downers Grove, IL: IVP Academic, 2009), 19.

4. Abraham J. Heschel, *The Prophets*, vol. 2 (New York: Harper & Row, 1962), 55; emphasis in the original.

5. Michael J. Williams, *The Prophet and His Message: Reading Old Testament Prophecy Today* (Phillipsburg, NJ: P & R, 2003), 16.

6. Williams, 17.

7. Williams, 18.

CHAPTER

Twelve

Deuteronomy in the New Testament

The teachings of the book of Deuteronomy are reflected not only in the Old Testament but also in the New Testament. Quotations from Deuteronomy are included throughout the entire New Testament[1] Additionally, there are many allusions, echoes, and hints from Deuteronomy in the New Testament's teachings. The intertextuality (how later authors apply Deuteronomy's material in their own writings) helps us understand the intended message of the book of Deuteronomy. Learning how biblical writers dialogue with Deuteronomy's instructions is a useful study. The four books of the Hebrew Bible that are most frequently quoted in the New Testament and also were used in the Qumran community are Genesis, Deuteronomy, Psalms, and Isaiah.[2]

Moses, as a model of religious authority in Israel, was seen in his prophetic ministry as a leader who pointed to the future and the true Prophet whom we need to obey—Jesus Christ (Deuteronomy 18:15; Hebrews 3:1–3). This idea is powerfully reflected in Peter's preaching at Pentecost (Acts 3:17–23). The New Testament authors believed that Moses was a real person and referred to him as such (for example, Matthew 17:3, 4; 22:24; Mark 1:44; 7:10; Luke 16:31; John 7:19; 9:28,

29; Acts 6:14; 7:20–44; Romans 5:14; 9:15; 10:5; Hebrews 3:5; 9:19; 11:24; Revelation 15:3). In the Gospel of John, Jesus explained to Nicodemus that He needed to be uplifted as the snake was lifted up by Moses in the desert (John 3:14) so "that everyone who believes" in Him as the Savior of the world "may have eternal life" (verse 15, NIV). Christ emphatically proclaimed, "If you believed Moses, you would believe me, for he wrote about me" (John 5:46, NIV).

When answering a difficult question about divorce, Jesus quoted Moses as the theological authority (Matthew 19:3–9). He understood the intention of each legislation and knew how to interpret and apply it correctly. In the discussion about divorce, the Pharisees referred back to Deuteronomy 24:1–4. Jesus countered them by explaining that "from the beginning it was not so" (Matthew 19:8, NKJV) and that this concession from God's Creation ideal was legislated only because of the people's stubbornness (Greek *sklerokardia* [verse 8]).

The significance of Deuteronomy for the New Testament can be highlighted by enumerating several additional facts:

1. Jesus Himself referred to the greatest commandment (Deuteronomy 6:5) in an open and transparent way. "You shall love the LORD your God with all your heart, with all your soul, and with all your mind" (Matthew 22:37, NKJV; compare Mark 12:30; Luke 10:27).
2. Deuteronomy centers on the Decalogue (Deuteronomy 5:6–21; Exodus 20:2–17) and its interpretation. Jesus further explained how to be a true disciple of God by showing acts of kindness, studying the Word of God, and praying (Luke 10; 11).
3. In Mark 12:29, Jesus quoted the Shema: "Hear, O Israel: The LORD our God, the LORD is one!" (Deuteronomy 6:4, NKJV) An emphasis on monotheism and statements against idolatry permeate Christ's teachings.
4. The apostle Paul drew important lessons for Christians from Israel's journey to the Promised Land. As end-time pilgrims, we

should pay close attention to his counsel because it is written for our admonition (1 Corinthians 10:1–12). The experiences of Israel are types, or examples, for us (verse 11) as we approach our entrance into the heavenly Canaan.

5. We should not add anything to God's revealed Word. This was emphasized to Israel and Joshua (Deuteronomy 4:2; 12:32; Joshua 1:7; Matthew 5:18; Revelation 22:18, 19).
6. Paul reminded believers to refrain from rage and leave revenge for injustices in God's hands. He quoted from Deuteronomy 32:35: " 'It is mine to avenge; I will repay,' says the Lord" (Romans 12:19, NIV).
7. Two songs of Moses will be sung by the redeemed on the sea of glass: one is a song of victory (Exodus 15), and the other is about God's character—His love, faithfulness, truth, justice, and holiness (Deuteronomy 32). The redeemed will sing the song of Moses and the Lamb on the new earth (Revelation 15:3, 4).

The underscoring of God's reliability in Deuteronomy 32 in the outstanding Song of Moses (verse 4) is a theme that is also picked up in the New Testament. It offers precious promises for the various tests, persecutions, trials, temptations, and hardships that we face in life. God will not let us go through that which we cannot endure, and He provides a way out of these distresses. Paul stated, "No temptation has overtaken you that is not common to man. God is faithful, and he will not let you be tempted beyond your ability, but with the temptation he will also provide the way of escape, that you may be able to endure it" (1 Corinthians 10:13, ESV). The NIrV presents the text in the following way: "You are tempted in the same way all other human beings are. God is faithful. He will not let you be tempted any more than you can take. But when you are tempted, God will give you a way out. Then you will be able to deal with it" (verse 13). Paul built on the assurance that we have in Christ. Jesus is always for His people, helping them with the difficulties of life.

Jesus Christ and the wilderness temptations

Significantly, the book of Deuteronomy played an important role in the life of Jesus Christ. He was deeply familiar with its message and loved to live according to its gospel. His devotion to the Word of God is evident in His reaction to the three wilderness temptations.

At the beginning of His public ministry, Christ was tempted by Satan (Matthew 4:1–11; compare Luke 4:1–13).[3] Satan wanted to divert Christ from His mission and overcome Him, so he came at a time when Jesus was vulnerable after forty days of fasting. He tried to distract Jesus from His main goal of dying victoriously for humanity. The devil wanted to confuse Him and turn Him away from His goal of saving humans and destroying evil. Satan tried to redirect Christ's focus and gain victory over Him, hoping to prevent Him from living a sinless life by resorting to the power that is unavailable to fragile human beings. Each of the three temptations was aimed at important aspects of Jesus' ministry.

First, Satan questioned the Messiahship of Jesus, challenging His close relationship with the heavenly Father. He wanted to cast doubt on Christ's conviction that He was the divine Son of man (Daniel 7:13), who came to live among humans and crush the head of the serpent (Genesis 3:15). He wanted Jesus to question His status as the Son of God (Daniel 3:25; Mark 1:1), who came to atone for sin, bring in everlasting righteousness, and die for humanity, thus saving humankind and fulfilling the Old Testament sacrificial system (Daniel 9:24–27).

Jesus was totally committed to the will of His Father. The culminating act of His obedience would be His death on the cross, but prior to that event, He needed to demonstrate His submission to God's law as the true criterion for being the Son of God. Jesus had to be victorious over temptations. In victory, He would stand in contrast to the Israelites who failed their test in the wilderness and to Adam who failed his test in the Garden of Eden (Genesis 3:1–7). Israel and Adam failed because they did not trust God and rebelled against His will.[4]

An exception to the pattern of human failure was Abraham. He passed his test of obedience (Genesis 22:1, 12, 16–18), even though he had failed on previous occasions.

Jesus overcame Satan's three crucial temptations by quoting texts from the book of Deuteronomy. Study carefully the biblical narrative in Matthew 4:3–11:

> The tempter came to him and said, "If you are the Son of God, tell these stones to become bread."
>
> Jesus answered, "It is written: 'Man shall not live on bread alone, but on every word that comes from the mouth of God.' "
>
> Then the devil took him to the holy city and had him stand on the highest point of the temple. "If you are the Son of God," he said, "throw yourself down. For it is written:
>
> > " 'He will command his angels concerning you,
> > and they will lift you up in their hands,
> > so that you will not strike your foot against a stone.' "
>
> Jesus answered him, "It is also written: 'Do not put the Lord your God to the test.' "
>
> Again, the devil took him to a very high mountain and showed him all the kingdoms of the world and their splendor. "All this I will give you," he said, "if you will bow down and worship me."
>
> Jesus said to him, "Away from me, Satan! For it is written: 'Worship the Lord your God, and serve him only.' "
>
> Then the devil left him, and angels came and attended him (NIV).

The first temptation. With this temptation, Satan was challenging Jesus to use the wrong means to prove He was the Son of God. According to the plan of redemption, Jesus Christ had to live on the earth as a fragile human being, fully obeying God's commands and living in complete dependence upon His Father. Satan wanted Jesus to transgress this principle and use His divine power to help Himself fulfill His mission. Satan was hoping to prove that it was not possible for humans to obey God and overcome their temptations, cementing his claim that God's commands were too severe and unjust, rendering them impossible to follow. Thus, the real purpose was to see whether Jesus could be victorious over sin and temptation when He set aside His Godhead privileges, relinquishing His divine power (Philippians 2:5–11). One of Jesus' great temptations was to utilize His divinity to help Himself (for example, changing stones into bread, which is not a temptation for humans) and perform miracles on His own behalf, thus escaping difficult circumstances rather than embracing a life of humility and sacrifice.

Satan came to Christ, seeking to divert Him and disprove that He was the Messiah, thus causing Him to fail in His mission to live a humble life in total dependence upon God and His Word. "If you are the Son of God, tell these stones to become bread" (Matthew 4:3, NIV). Jesus reacted with a clear "It is written." He was victorious in this encounter with Satan because of the Word of God. Quoting from Deuteronomy 8:3, Jesus overcame the temptation: "Man does not live on bread alone but on every word that comes from the mouth of the LORD" (NIV; compare Matthew 4:4).

The second temptation. It was a huge temptation for Jesus to publicly demonstrate that He was truly the Son of God. Testing God from the top of the temple was an inducement to avoid a life of humble service and self-denial and the need to disguise His true identity. In the second wilderness temptation, Jesus responded with another quotation from Deuteronomy: "You shall not put the LORD your God to the test" (Deuteronomy 6:16, ESV). This temptation was also a battle over the right interpretation of the Scriptures. Satan incorrectly used them (quoting Psalm 91:11, 12), but Jesus rightly applied them, using sound interpretation by considering the context and the purpose of the biblical texts. He was victorious for the second time.

The third temptation. Finally, Satan claimed that he was the prince of this world and had the authority to give the earthly kingdoms to Jesus without any struggle. Only one condition must be met: Jesus needed to bow down before Lucifer and accept him as the legal ruler of the earth. Christ refused the offer and firmly decided that He would go through the fiercest battles with evil to completely crush all of Satan's claims and prove him a liar. In other words, Jesus could have had it all without sacrifice, pain, and death. He only needed to acknowledge Satan as the rightful ruler over the earth.

In His response to this third temptation, Jesus clearly recognized who was behind these attempts to divert Him from His mission, answering: "Away from me, Satan! For it is written: 'Worship the Lord your God, and serve him only' " (Matthew 4:10, NIV). This is a quotation from Deuteronomy 6:13: "Fear the LORD your God, serve him only" (NIV). (*Fearing* and *worshiping* the Lord are synonymous terms.)

A careful reading of the three wilderness temptations shows that Jesus defeated Satan by quoting and applying three biblical texts from the book of Deuteronomy. Christ knew its message well, and at the right time, He resisted the temptations to ease His difficult mission on this earth: (1) Jesus would not use His divine power to help Himself in suffering and conquering evil; (2) He would not use His popularity and miracles to divert Himself from His mission to die for humanity in order to save us; and (3) He would not bow down before Satan to validate his rebellion against God and His will. Christ came to defeat Satan through His weakness, total dedication, and complete obedience to His Father.

The three temptations were about the desire of the flesh (the first temptation), the pride or arrogance of life (the second temptation), and the desire of the eyes (the third temptation). John wrote, "For all that is in the world—the desires of the flesh and the desires of the eyes and pride of life—is not from the Father but is from the world" (1 John 2:16, ESV). These three wilderness temptations were also negations of the greatest commandment of love: "You shall love the LORD your God with all your heart and with all your soul and with all your might" (Deuteronomy 6:5, ESV).

How is it with us? Do we live every day by God's Word? Do we live lives of dependence upon His goodness, enjoying His presence and guidance? Let us take into our hearts the encouraging words of Peter and pray that they will be our daily experience: "But grow in the grace and knowledge of our Lord and Savior Jesus Christ. To him be glory both now and forever" (2 Peter 3:18, NIV)!

---

1. See especially (1) Deuteronomy 1:16, 17; 16:19; John 7:24; James 2:1; (2) Deuteronomy 4:2; 12:32; Matthew 5:18; Revelation 22:18, 19; (3) Deuteronomy 4:7; James 4:8; (4) Deuteronomy 4:29–31; 31:6; Hebrews 8:8b; 11:6; 13:5; (5) Deuteronomy 5:5; Galatians 3:19; (6) Deuteronomy 7:8; 1 John 4:10; (7) Deuteronomy 9:7, 24; 10:16; Acts 7:51; (8) Deuteronomy 9:15, 19; Hebrews 12:18; (9) Deuteronomy 10:17; Acts 10:34; 1 Timothy 6:15; (10) Deuteronomy 13:13; 2 Corinthians 6:15; (11) Deuteronomy 4:2; 26:19; 28:9; 1 Peter 2:9; (12) Deuteronomy 15:11; Matthew 26:11; John 12:8; (13) Deuteronomy 16:20; 1 Timothy 6:11; (14) Deuteronomy 17:6; 19:15; Matthew 18:16; John 8:17; 2 Corinthians 13:1; Hebrews 10:28; (15) Deuteronomy 18:15; Acts 3:22; 7:37; John 1:21; 6:14; Matthew 21:11; (16) Deuteronomy 18:16; Hebrews 12:19; (17) Deuteronomy 18:19; Luke 10:16; John 12:48; Acts 3:23; (18) Deuteronomy 18:18; John 12:49; (19) Deuteronomy 19:19; 17:7; 1 Corinthians 5:13; (20) Deuteronomy 19:21; Matthew 5:38; (21) Deuteronomy 21:6; Matthew 27:24; (22) Deuteronomy 21:23; Galatians 3:13; (23) Deuteronomy 22:22; John 8:4; (24) Deuteronomy 23:25; Matthew 12:1; (25) Deuteronomy 24:1; Matthew 5:31; 19:3; (26) Deuteronomy 24:14; James 5:4; (27) Deuteronomy 25:3; 2 Corinthians 11:24; (28) Deuteronomy 25:4; 1 Corinthians 9:9; 1 Timothy 5:18; (29) Deuteronomy 25:5; Matthew 22:24; (30) Deuteronomy 27:26; Galatians 3:10; (31) Deuteronomy 29:4; Romans 11:8; (32) Deuteronomy 29:18; Hebrews 12:15; (33) Deuteronomy 30:6; Romans 2:29; (34) Deuteronomy 30:12–14; Romans 10:6–8; (35) Deuteronomy 31:26; Romans 3:19; (36) Deuteronomy 32:21; Romans 10:19; (37) Deuteronomy 32:35; Romans 12:19; Hebrews 10:30; and (38) Deuteronomy 32:43; Romans 15:10.

2. Martin Abegg Jr., Peter Flint, and Eugene Ulrich, trans., *The Dead Sea Scrolls Bible: The Oldest Known Bible Translated for the First Time Into English* (New York: HarperSanFrancisco, 1999), xvii, 3.

3. The sequence of the second and the third temptations are reversed in Luke's narrative in comparison to Matthew's account.

4. Jiří Moskala, "Origin of Sin and Salvation According to Genesis 3: A Theology of Sin," in *Salvation: Contours of Adventist Soteriology*, ed. Martin F. Hanna, Darius W. Jankiewicz, and John W. Reeve (Berrien Springs, MI: Andrews University Press, 2018), 119–143.

CHAPTER

Thirteen

The Resurrection of Moses

In the middle of the last chapter of the book of Deuteronomy, we read, "And Moses the servant of the LORD died there in Moab, as the LORD had said" (Deuteronomy 34:5, NIV). Moses died in a foreign country while on a pilgrimage to a new home. He did not reach it, but a better land than the Promised Land awaited him.

The death of Moses

The book of Deuteronomy is the biography of Moses' last two months of life, ending with the story of his death. But his death was premature. It was not caused by old age, because at 120 years old, he was still in good health. No, he died because God had barred him from entering the Promised Land.

Moses understood this and engaged in three exhortative sermons to encourage the people to fear the Lord and be faithful to Him. He appointed Joshua as the new leader who would guide the people of God into the Promised Land, taught them a special song, and pronounced a final blessing upon them.

It is interesting that God is depicted in the last chapter of the book of Deuteronomy with only one name—the Lord (Yahweh). Yahweh is the proper name for God and is used seven times in this chapter. Yahweh is the Lord of His people—an immanent God. Yahweh is a personal, close God; He is the God of the covenant who intervenes in our lives. So it was proper that God was intimately involved in Moses' death.

The greatest tribute to Moses' legacy is given in the epitaph about him in the last three verses of Deuteronomy: "Since then, no prophet has risen in Israel like Moses, whom the LORD knew face to face, who did all those signs and wonders the LORD sent him to do in Egypt—to Pharaoh and to all his officials and to his whole land. For no one has ever shown the mighty power or performed the awesome deeds that Moses did in the sight of all Israel" (verses 10–12, NIV). What an outstanding summary of his life! Moses was faithful to his call and ministry. He fulfilled God's task with excellence and distinction, becoming a model of dedicated prophetic ministry.

As Moses was climbing Mount Nebo, he knew he would die on that mountain. On the summit, the Lord showed him the whole Promised Land (verses 1–4). The vast panorama lay before him. Not only did he see the beautiful land flourishing under God's blessing, but he was also shown the painful future of God's people leading up to the first advent of Christ. Then he viewed the triumphant end of the great controversy and the establishment of the new earth, even more splendid than the Promised Land.[1] The biblical text testifies that God Himself buried His friend: "He [the antecedent is the Lord] buried him in Moab" (verse 6, NIV) in an unknown place so that the location of his burial would not become a venerated pilgrimage site, paving the way for idolatrous practices.

The book of Deuteronomy emphatically calls people to obedience. Obedience is the only proper response to God's covenant of faithfulness and love. Through his words, Moses sought to motivate people to respond to the Lord's care and follow their merciful God. "Obedience in the spirit of love, flowing from a blessed and enjoyed relationship with Jehovah, is the demand made of His people. . . . He redeemed them out of the house of bondage, carried them through the wilderness, guided them, gave them food, sustained them." Their response to His tender, loving care was "to be expressed by obedience." The principle of the book of Deuteronomy is "obedience to Jehovah and His Word in the spirit of love and godly fear."[2] Unfortunately, Moses himself did not obey God on a special occasion, and he had to confront the bitter consequences of his unbelief and impatience.

As described in Numbers 20, Moses' cardinal sin occurred at Kadesh when the people complained and quarreled due to a lack of water. Because the rock represented Christ (1 Corinthians 10:4), the Lord told Moses to speak to the rock in order to bring water out of it (Numbers 20:8). What happened then was the most tragic misstep in Moses' entire ministry. He, along with Aaron (verse 12; Deuteronomy 32:51), confronted the problem but became irritated and impatient with the people. " 'Hear now, you rebels! Must we bring water for you out of this rock?' Then Moses lifted his hand and struck the rock twice with his rod; and water came out abundantly, and the congregation and their animals drank" (Numbers 20:10, 11, NKJV). God was not pleased with Moses' clear disregard for His instructions. "Because you did not believe Me, to hallow Me in the eyes of the children of Israel, therefore you shall not bring this assembly into the land which I have given them" (verse 12, NKJV). Ellen White gives the following insight into this situation:

> His lack of patience and self-control was evident. . . .
>
> . . . [Moses' and Aaron's] own faith in the fulfillment of God's promise had been shaken by the murmuring and rebellion of the people.[3]

Even when confronting deep disobedience, we should speak with patience and tact: "This accusation was true [Moses' accusation that the people were rebelling], but even truth is not to be spoken in passion or impatience."[4]

Moses' sin is described in Deuteronomy 32:51 from two angles. The Lord defined it as follows: (1) "you broke faith [Hebrew *ma'al*, meaning act faithlessly, be unfaithful, betray] with me in the presence of the Israelites"; and (2) "you did not uphold my holiness among the Israelites" (NIV). His public sin was thus twofold: (1) Moses did not trust that the Lord was able to fulfill His promise by only the spoken word and consequently broke faith by not obeying God's command (1 Samuel 14:33; Malachi 2:11); and (2) he did not uphold God's holy presence among the Israelites (God's holiness is His presence [Exodus 3:4–6]). The gift of water was not Moses' performance; it was not about him but about God. God characterized Moses' failure in transparent terms: "You rebelled against my command" (Numbers 20:24, NIV). Moses neglected to give God the glory for this miracle and forfeited entrance to the Promised Land.

Three times in his first speech to Israel, Moses expressed his deep grief and disappointment that he could not enter the Promised Land (Deuteronomy 1:37; 3:23–27; 4:21–24). He pleaded with the Lord to allow him to go into the land beyond the Jordan, but the Lord's answer was negative (Deuteronomy 3:26). This provides a clear lesson for us: everyone needs to obey the Lord and His Word—leaders as well as members of the community of faith. There are no exceptions; leaders are also under the law. Even though it was the desire of his heart, Moses was deprived of this privilege because he dishonored God. The biblical text gives an explicit reason for this denial: Moses robbed God of His holiness before the people. God treats everyone fairly; with Him, there is no favoritism (see Romans 2:11). Ellen White states that if Moses had not committed this sin, "he would have entered the Promised Land, and would have been translated to heaven without seeing death."[5]

The legacy of Moses is alive today because he made God the center of his life and service to His people a priority. God used him in a powerful way because he put all distractions aside and allowed God to lead his life. His memory remains with us for this reason, and we can learn from him. This is why we follow the advice and admonishment found in the book of Hebrews: "Remember your leaders, those who spoke to you the word of God. Consider the outcome of their way of life, and imitate their faith" (Hebrews 13:7, ESV). Memories of the faithful will never be lost because the deeds of those who fear the Lord are written in the book of remembrance (Malachi 3:16).

The resurrection of Moses

Moses' death was not a tragedy because he died in the blessed hope and with a firm faith in God. In addition, he did not stay in the grave long because God, who is Life and is the Giver of life, resurrected him. Incredible! While the closing verses of Deuteronomy report Moses' death, the New Testament testifies to his resurrection. Jude specifically mentions how Satan claimed that Moses belonged to him because of his sin, hoping to keep him in the tomb as his trophy (Jude 9). But God forgave Moses' impatience and lack of trust, just as He forgives our sins and trespasses when we repent and confess them honestly and sincerely (1 John 1:7, 9). No evil forces can stop God and hold Him back; when God is for us, who can be against us? The resurrection of Moses proves that sinners can experience resurrection when they ask for forgiveness and renew their trust in God.

The story is simple but changes the world. Jesus Christ Himself resurrected Moses from his resting place on Mount Nebo. The biblical account reads, "But even the archangel Michael, when he was disputing with the devil about the body of Moses, did not himself dare to condemn him for slander but said, 'The Lord rebuke you!' " (Jude 9, NIV). Historically, Moses' resurrection was the first one performed by Jesus Christ! A dead person was raised to life. It is no wonder that Satan was shocked when he realized that he had completely lost his cause.

The God of Moses is the Source of life. Because God is alive, Moses could live. The Gospel of Matthew testifies that Moses and Elijah (who did not die or even taste the bitterness of death [2 Kings 2]) were present with Jesus at the time of His transfiguration, encouraging Him on the journey toward His death (Matthew 17:3, 4). So when we speak about the death of Moses, we should focus on his legacy and the good news of his resurrection. This gives us hope as we look forward to the day of resurrection at Christ's second coming.

Hope of resurrection in the Old Testament

The hope of the resurrection is strong in the Old Testament, beginning with Job and culminating with Daniel. In between, several authors also testify to it. Let us briefly review the main texts related to the hope of resurrection:

1. Job 19:25–27. I do not know of a more powerful and more outstanding text on the personal certainty of resurrection than that from Job. Job 19:25–27 is a stunning and eloquently expressed confession of faith. These verses contain one of the most beautiful expressions of hope in a bodily resurrection. This is a declaration that one can find engraved on many Christian tombs. Job's powerful statement that he will see God in his flesh after death is the oldest in the Bible and sets the tone for this incredible hope of what God will do at the end of this earth's history. Job states, "I know that my Redeemer lives." He knows his God and that He is alive, and he calls Him a "Redeemer" (Hebrew *goel*, meaning kinsman-redeemer, defender, vindicator, protector), as Boaz was for Ruth (Ruth 4:14). Job continues with the assurance that his Redeemer "in the end . . . will stand on the earth" (Job 19:25, NIV) to resurrect him to new life. Regrettably, people usually only know and quote verse 25, but what follows is equally crucial:

"And after my skin has been destroyed,
  yet in my flesh I will see God;
I myself will see him
  with my own eyes—I, and not another.
  How my heart yearns within me!" (verses 26, 27, NIV).

Notice the personal tone of Job's solemn declaration: *I, my, myself, own*. He firmly believes in his heart that in his flesh, with his own eyes, he will see God even though he will die and his skin will be destroyed. This personal assurance of a future resurrection day cannot be expressed in a better and more emphatic way.

2. Psalm 16:9, 10. These verses state the following:

> Therefore my heart is glad and my tongue rejoices;
> my body also will rest secure,
> because you will not abandon me to the realm of the dead [*sheol*, meaning grave, death],
> nor will you let your faithful one see decay (Psalm 16:9, 10, NIV).

The Hebrew term *sheol* should be translated as "grave" here as it is in many other passages. This term is found sixty-six times in the Hebrew Bible, and in the majority of cases, its meaning is synonymous with the grave. Both the wicked and the righteous descend to *sheol* (Genesis 37:35; 42:38; 44:29, 31; Numbers 16:30, 33; 1 Kings 2:6, 9; Job 21:13; Psalms 49:15; 89:48; Ecclesiastes 9:10; Isaiah 14:9, 11, 15; 38:10; Ezekiel 31:15–17). In addition, the Lord redeems the faithful from *sheol* (Hosea 13:14), no one can hide from God in *sheol* (Psalm 139:8; Amos 9:2), and there is no work or other activity in *sheol* (Ecclesiastes 9:10). Nowhere in the Bible is *sheol* described as the shadowy underworld where the dead live or where human souls or spirits continue their existence. The word *sheol* is a designation for the grave—the place of the dead (see, for example, the consistency of the 1984 NIV translation where the word *sheol* is translated as "grave" fifty-seven times but also as "death" six times, "realm of the dead" once, "deepest depths" once, and "depth" once). David rejoices that he will rest in peace after death and will not be forgotten by the Lord but resurrected to a new life and will not experience lasting destruction (Hebrew *shakhat*, meaning destruction, corruption, decay, pit).

This text transcends the experience of David and has a deeper Messianic meaning. The "faithful one" (Hebrew *khasid*, meaning devoted, faithful One, Holy One)—that is, the Messiah Jesus Christ—will not rot in His tomb, and His body will not decay because He will be resurrected after resting three days (counted inclusively) in the grave (*sheol*). The New Testament quotes this text as a prophetic announcement of Christ's resurrection (Acts 2:25–28; 13:35).

3. Psalm 49:9–15. The psalmist presents a contrast between the general fate of people and the reward of the righteous. On the one hand, people will die and go to their graves (*sheol*) because they will not "live on forever and not see decay [*shakhat*]" (Psalm 49:9, NIV; compare Psalms 16:10; 17:15). On the other hand, those who love and obey the Lord will have a different destiny. The poet declares, "God will redeem [Hebrew *padah*, meaning ransom, redeem] me from the realm of the dead [*sheol*, grave]; he will surely take me to himself [Hebrew *laqakh*, meaning receive, take up]" (Psalm 49:15, NIV). The NLT translators interpret the Hebrew text in a powerful way: "He [God] will snatch me from the power of the grave."

4. Psalm 71:20. This verse states the following:

> Though you have made me see troubles,
>   many and bitter,
>   you will restore my life again;
> from the depths of the earth
>   you will again bring me up (Psalm 71:20, NIV).

This psalm is a prayer for God's help in the psalmist's old age. The Lord has been with him from birth and has done great things for him, so he asks for God's protection from his enemies. God not only restores physical strength and health but also has the power to resurrect. The psalmist believes and hopes that God will bring him up (Hebrew *'alah*, meaning go up, ascend) from "the depths [Hebrew *tehom*, meaning literally abyss, deep] of the earth," which may be a figurative description of the grave. Thus, this poetic imagery hints at a physical resurrection. The NLT translators render this phrase into the following hope: "You will restore me to life again and lift me up from the depths of the earth."

5. Psalm 73:23, 24. Asaph, in his existential quest for understanding the puzzles of life regarding the prosperity of the wicked and the suffering of the righteous, concludes that it is God who holds him and guides him. God secures his future and will resurrect him to eternal life: "You hold me by my right hand. You guide me with your counsel, and afterward you will take me into glory" (Psalm 73:23, 24, NIV). God gives meaning to the present life; moreover, He secures our future even after death. The verb for being "taken up" is *laqakh*, and this verb is used in the story of Enoch when God took him up (Genesis 5:24) as well as in the narrative of Elijah, who was also taken up to heaven (2 Kings 2:3, 9; another verb is also used—namely *'alah*, go up—in 2 Kings 2:1, 11).

6. Isaiah 26:19. The prophet Isaiah in his so-called little apocalypse presents the hope of resurrection and announces it boldly:

> Your dead shall live; their bodies shall rise.
>   You who dwell in the dust, awake and sing for joy!
> For your dew is a dew of light,
>   and the earth will give birth to the dead (Isaiah 26:19, ESV).

There is a glorious hope and bright future for those who stay with the Lord. This is a very explicit verse about a physical resurrection from death. Years later, Daniel roots his statement regarding the resurrection in Isaiah's proclamation.

7. Daniel 12:2, 12. The prophet Daniel points to a day of resurrection: "Multitudes who sleep in the dust of the earth will awake: some to everlasting life, others to shame and everlasting contempt" (Daniel 12:2, NIV). God's Old Testament revelation culminates with this declaration. Death is compared to sleep, and those who are dead will be resurrected: those who served the Lord will receive eternal life, but the wicked will be condemned to eternal death.

God also assures Daniel that he will be resurrected to new life at the very end of time: "As for you, go your way till the end. You will rest, and then at the end of the days you will rise to receive your allotted inheritance" (verse 13, NIV). Death is like a rest from faithful labor. But then will come the sweet inheritance—eternal life with the Lord.

8. Jonah 2:2. Jonah's stay for three days in the belly of a big fish is an allusion to the resurrection. Jonah defines this experience as being in *sheol*, meaning in a grave (Jonah 2:2). After three days and three nights, he was brought to a new life when he was vomited out of this *sheol.* In a prayer, he states,

> "I went down to the land
> whose bars closed upon me forever;
> yet you brought up my life from the pit,
> O Lord my God" (verse 6, ESV).

Jesus compared His stay in the grave and His resurrection to Jonah's experience (Matthew 12:40).

9. Hosea 6:2. The prophet Hosea speaks about Israel's spiritual revival and return to the Lord in terms of raising the people from death to new life. The imagery of resurrection is used to explain this new life for God's people.

Hope of resurrection in the New Testament

Many New Testament authors affirm their belief in the resurrection in powerful ways. Due to a lack of space, I will only note the principal passages affirming the magnificent doctrine of the resurrection: Matthew 22:32, 33; John 5:25–29; 11:25; 1 Corinthians 15:12–20, 51–57; 1 Thessalonians 4:13–17; Revelation 20:4–6, 11–15.

I conclude our reflection on the resurrection with the outstanding, affirmative words of Jesus: "I am the resurrection and the life. He who believes in Me, though he may die, he shall live" (John 11:25, NKJV). John also records the following teaching of Jesus: "Do not be amazed at this, for a time is coming when all who are in their graves will hear his voice and come out—those who have done what is good will rise to live, and those who have done what is evil will rise to be condemned" (John 5:28, 29, NIV). In the presence of the Prince of Life, there is no room for death (John 3:16; Revelation 21:4).

---

1. For these insights, study carefully Ellen G. White, *Patriarchs and Prophets* (Mountain View, CA: Pacific Press®, 1958), 469–480.
2. Arno C. Gaebelein, introduction to "The Book of Deuteronomy," in *Arno Gaebelein's Annotated Bible*, accessed February 21, 2021, https://www.studylight.org/commentaries/eng/gab/deuteronomy.html.
3. White, *Patriarchs and Prophets*, 417; for further insights and lessons, see also 411–421.
4. White, 417.
5. White, 478.

Appendix

The Literary Structure of Deuteronomy

Deuteronomy is an exceptional work of a genius. Moses, under the inspiration of the Holy Spirit, deliberately put God's revelation into an outstanding literary structure. The book is written in a complex manner because Moses intertwined three structures to form one document. He was enabled to combine different literary genres—history, narrative, legislation, poetry, song, admonishments, blessings, curses, and sermons—producing a united whole. Thus, three structures are mingled together as follows:

1. The rhetorical structure, with the three speeches or sermons (Deuteronomy 1:6–4:43; 4:44–28:68; 29; 30)
2. The covenant structure, with its six parts (according to the literary pattern of the covenants of the time): preamble (1:1–6a), historical prologue (1:6b–4:43), stipulations (4:44–26:19), blessings and curses (27:1–30:20), witnesses (30:19; 31:19), and special provisions of the covenant (31:9–13)
3. The exposition of each of the Ten Commandments in the central part of the book—namely, in the second sermon (first principles are clarified in chapters 5–11, and then each commandment is explained in chapters 12–26)

This threefold structure strengthens the unity of the book. To this, the transition of leadership from Moses to Joshua is added (chapter 31) as well as Moses' song (chapter 32) and his concluding blessings for Israel (chapter 33). Of course, the narrative regarding the death of Moses (chapter 34) is included in the final composition of Deuteronomy. I put these rhetorical, covenantal, and expositional themes of the Decalogue structures into one overall architectural outline to see the beautiful result in the following seven parts of the book:

The principal title of the book: Choose life—love, obey, and fear the Lord

I. Introduction—the preamble of the covenant (1:1–6a): the background for the whole book and the first presentation of the Lord.

II. Moses' first speech or address—the historical prologue of the covenant (1:6b–4:43).

- A. Seven crucial reminders: seven characteristic stories from the time of the pilgrimage from Horeb (Sinai) to the Jordan:
    1. God's promise and the appointment of leaders at Horeb (1:6b–18).
    2. Journey from Mount Horeb to Kadesh, sending the spies, and the rebellion against the Lord at Kadesh (1:19–46).
    3. Wandering in the wilderness around the hill country of Seir and the Transjordan—Israel commanded not to fight with Edom, Moab, and Ammon (2:1–23).
    4. Victory over Sihon, king of Heshbon—the conquest of the Transjordan (2:24–37).
    5. Victory over Og, king of Bashan—the conquest of the Transjordan (3:1–11).
    6. Distribution of the land to the two and a half Transjordan tribes and the command to them (3:12–20).
    7. Moses' encouragement to Joshua to conquer the land, and his plea to the Lord to enter the Promised Land (3:21–29).

B. Climax: "Hear, O Israel"—exhortation to obey and trust the Lord, along with practical consequences for Israel (4:1–40).
C. Appendix: The three cities of refuge (4:41–43).

III. Moses' second speech or address—the exposition of the law, exhortations, warnings, and blessings and curses of the covenant (4:44–28:68).
A. Covenant stipulations (4:44–26:19).
1. The foundational principles and the spirit of the law (4:44–11:32).
a) The proclamation of the Decalogue and exhortation to live it (4:44–5:33).
b) The summary of the Decalogue and what it involves: "Love the Lord your God" (6:1–25).
c) The possession of the land, separation from idolatry, and God's love for His people (7:1–26).
d) "You shall remember the Lord your God"—encouragement and warning (8:1–20).
e) Warning against self-righteousness and Israel's previous failures (9:1–10:11).
f) "Fear the Lord your God," and keep His requirements (10:12–22).
g) Israel's responsibility, encouragement to serve Him, and the basic blessings and curses (11:1–32).
2. The expansion of the Decalogue (12–26).
a) The first two commandments—worship (12:1–32).
(1) True love and false worship (12:1–4).
(2) Right place and genuine, authorized worship (12:5–14).
(3) Secular and sacrificial slaughter (12:15–28).
(4) Abhor pagan worship (12:29–32).
b) The third commandment—name of God (13:1–14:29).
(1) Warning against false prophets and their punishment (13:1–18).
(2) Conduct of the holy people—marking the difference

between clean and unclean foods (14:1–21).
- (3) Tithe (14:22–29).
- c) The fourth commandment—Sabbath (15:1–16:17).
  - (1) The year of release: canceling debts and the liberation of Hebrew slaves (15:1–18).
  - (2) Firstborn animals and the three main feasts (15:19–16:17).
- d) The fifth commandment—authority (16:18–18:22).
  - (1) Justice and the choice of a king (16:18–17:20).
  - (2) The rights of the priests and Levites, and the true and the false prophet (18:1–22).
- e) The sixth commandment—homicide (19:1–22:8).
  - (1) Laws related to murder and cities of refuge (19:1–14).
  - (2) Laws related to witnesses (19:15–21).
  - (3) Concerning future wars (20:1–20).
  - (4) Atonement for an unsolved murder (21:1–9).
  - (5) Various instructions regarding defending or executing people and protecting life (21:10–22:8).
- f) The seventh commandment—adultery (22:9–23:18).
  - (1) Mixing the wrong things together (22:9–12).
  - (2) Sanctity of marriage and sexual sins (22:13–30).
  - (3) The Lord's congregation: its constitution and holiness (23:1–18).
- g) The eighth commandment—theft (23:19–24:7).
  - (1) Concerning interest, keeping one's word, and sharing the results of a harvest (23:19–25).
  - (2) Concerning protections for an accused woman, the newly married, the debtor, and a life (24:1–7).
- h) The ninth commandment—false charges (24:8–25:4).
  - (1) Various laws of protection for the community, the employee, and the innocent (24:8–16).
  - (2) Responsibility of protecting the weak, poor, offenders, and animals (24:17–25:4).

i) The tenth commandment—coveting (25:5–26:15).
   (1) Brother's wife, dishonesty, and the Amalekites (25:5–19).
   (2) Firstfruits, tithe, and prayer (26:1–15).
j) Appeal to renew the covenant (26:16–19).

B. The blessings and curses of the covenant (27:1–28:68).

IV. Moses' third speech or address—further exposition of the blessings and curses, the ultimate appeal, and enumeration of witnesses (29:1–30:20).
   A. Moses' final charge to Israel—the repetition of the covenant blessings and the restated curses (29:1–29).
   B. Return to the Lord your God and receive prosperity: the Lord is your life, so choose life (30:1–20).
      1. Witnesses (30:19; see also 31:19, 26, 28).

V. Preparation for the future: leadership transition and Moses' final actions and words (31–33).
   A. Leadership handover from Moses to Joshua and the Lord's Word to Moses (31:1–8).
   B. Special provision of the covenant (31:9–13).
   C. Israel's rebellion predicted (31:14–22).
   D. The Lord's address to Joshua (31:23).
   E. Moses' instructions about his book of the law (31:24–29).
   F. The last Song of Moses (32).
   G. The blessing of the tribes of Israel by Moses (33).

VI. The death of Moses (34:1–8).
   A. Moses' climb up Mount Nebo, and God's closing speech to Moses (34:1–4).
   B. Death and burial of Moses (34:5–8).

VII. The Epilogue (34:9–12).

Praise the Lord for such a magnificent message, delivered in a perfectly organized way! Let us familiarize ourselves with Deuteronomy's content, because in this way, we will learn not only about

God's amazing love but also how to love, admire, obey, worship, serve, fear, and follow the Lord out of gratitude for who He is, what He has done, is doing, and will do. To Him only belongs the glory (Psalm 115:1; Jeremiah 9:23, 24; Ephesians 3:20, 21; Jude 24, 25)!